# The Cowman Says It Salty

# The Cowman

Illustrated by VIC DONAHUE

# Says It SALTY

## Ramon F. Adams

THE UNIVERSITY OF ARIZONA PRESS
Tucson, Arizona

*About the Author . . .*

RAMON F. ADAMS for many years has been a collector — of words, not things — and this book is the result of his years of gathering and recording the cowboy's words and phrases. A native Texan, he first became interested in the language of the cowboy during his youth when he lived in the suburbs of Houston near a dying cattle trail. After some years devoted to the serious study of the violin and playing in Dallas movie theater orchestras during the silent-picture days, he made the collecting of this unique cowboy language his life's work. The author of numerous books and bibliographies on the subject, as well as magazine articles, and introductions and chapters for the books of others, he has traveled widely in his quest for material. In 1971 at the age of eighty-two he was still writing and pursuing his hobby from his home in Dallas.

THE UNIVERSITY OF ARIZONA PRESS

I.S.B.N.-0-8165-0311-7
L.C. No.-73-174805

*to*

JOHN D. GILCHRIESE

*a real historian
and loyal friend*

# Foreword

IT IS MOST FITTING that in the Indian summer of his life, the distinguished American author and bibliographer, Ramon F. Adams, would write this book embracing and gathering the vernacular of a vigorous people scattered on the face of the American West. This land — inhospitable, passive, violent — repulsed the timid, challenged the bold, and refuted the cowardly.

Ranching in the West was a pastoral occupation dominated by a resplendent variety of cattlemen whose ancestry and language were as varied as their manners, morals and customs. The drover — now called cowboy — was a skillful, colorful, often enigmatic individual who plied his skill and knowledge from the Missouri to the Pacific Ocean with his counterparts, the Mexican *vaquero* and the fur-chapped cowboy exposed to the harsh Canadian winters. A variety of languages ranging from the precise speech of the English financier who dreamed of success with the purchase of a large ranch somewhere on the Great Plains, to the descriptive dialogue of the French *entrepreneur,* to the unmistakable Americanisms of the resolute Yankee and the romantic symbolism of the Spanish language — the basic tongue of the cattle industry — to the rolling speech of the Scots with its Gaelic origin, and the drawling rhythm of the Southerner met and mingled harmoniously. From this admixture, forged upon the anvil of necessity, came idioms of speech — terse, salty, earthy, and beautifully descriptive of the time and the place, the prevailing conditions and the majesty of the land. The cowboy, the cattleman, the Westerner, thus composed a language that suited himself, unmindful that he might be accused of corrupting grammatical form in choosing to "say it salty." If this new language supplanted his basic vocabulary, the cowboy and cattleman were undoubtedly unaware of it. That he chose a direct route of expression, couched in the rhythmic cadence of his life, is completely understandable.

In a land of simple hospitality, strangers might be suspect, curiosity a crime, and sentimentality too revealing. The Western man, associated with cattle, dust, distance and loneliness, sought to say what he must in the way that suited him best. Formal education was often alien to the man of action. It is readily understandable why he embraced a lingo pithy and precise to his ear.

Ramon F. Adams, attuned by virtue of eight decades, has lived, spoken and written in two worlds — one the measured meter of the academic world, and the other where he sympathetically listened to and recorded for posterity the indigenous magnificence of a marvelously innovated and acquired pattern of folk-speech.

The cowboy was neither inarticulate nor verbose; he was the perfect example of action and expression, able to delineate his world by saying it as he saw it, while rapturously enjoying it to the hilt.

In this learned and sympathetic account, the cowman and his cohorts are forever enshrined by the incomparable knowledge of Ramon F. Adams. Long may the salty expressions of the cowman exist in a world of scientific jargon that tends to remove us from that world of man, beast and unfettered expression, always timeless and relevant to the heritage of this great nation.

JOHN D. GILCHRIESE
*Field Historian*
*The University of Arizona*

# Contents

# Introduction

THE COWBOY was — and is — picturesque, not only in clothing, in manner and mode of life, but in speech; and we owe him a debt of gratitude for many things, not the least of which is his contribution to our language. Any manner of life with a rule and flavor of its own strong enough to put a new dress on a man's body will put new speech in his mouth; and an idiom derived from the stress of his life was soon spoken by the cowboy.

I became interested in his lingo in the early 1900s, being vividly impressed by his strikingly apt and vigorous figures of speech when privileged to listen to his conversations while among his own kind. Even though I have written several books upon this subject, I make no claim that the ground has been covered completely, for with every conversation new metaphors are born. But I do hope I am able to give the reader a deeper understanding of the man through his speech. My hobby of a long lifetime has been collecting this lingo, and my purpose in writing this book is with the hope his unique speech will not be lost, but preserved for future generations.

Feeling his carefree good humor we, in turn, forget the worry and strain of our own hectic existence. Unlike us, to the cowboy money meant nothing. He would work hard for thirty dollars a month, then spend it all with his characteristic free-heartedness in an hour of relaxation. All that seriously concerned him was plenty to eat, a good horse to ride, a saddle for his throne — and he was king.

Living in isolated groups, visiting but little among themselves, rarely going to town, shy and timid as a result of long days of solitude, the cowboy developed his own speech. His words, phrases and customs, therefore, became community property, his language a dialect of his own.

But isolation made him an individual. Perhaps the strength and originality in his speech is due to the solitude, the nearness of the stars, the bigness of the country, and the far horizons, all of which gave him a chance to catalog each detail and store it away in his mind for future use. Wide spaces "don't breed chatter-boxes." On his long and lonely rides, he was not forced to listen to scandal and idle gossip that dwarf a man's mind. Quite frequently he had no one to talk to but a horse that could not talk back.

Sententiousness being a characteristic of the range, it became a social obligation to speak in terse terms, and, when speaking a sentence, in the words of the cowboy, to "bobtail 'er and fill 'er with meat."

Many of his technical terms and slang have been preserved in my *Western Words,* and a number of his unique figures of speech have been recorded in such of my books as *Cowboy Lingo, Western Words, Come An' Get It,* and *The Old-Time Cowhand.* These, together with many not included in those books, are now placed in this work in an effort to preserve them for posterity all under one cover. If this effort has been of interest and of value to any one reader, I shall feel amply repaid for my endeavor. I hope, however, this book will find a permanent place on the shelf with his other published lore because speech is an important phase of man's avocation.

RAMON F. ADAMS

OTHER BOOKS BY RAMON F. ADAMS

*Cowboy Lingo* (Boston, 1936)

*Western Words: A Dictionary of Range, Cow Camp and Trail* (Norman, 1944)

*Charles M. Russell, the Cowboy Artist* (Pasadena, 1948)

*Come an' Get It: The Story of the Old Cowboy Cook* (Norman, 1952)

*The Best of the American Cowboy* (compiler and editor) (Norman, 1957)

*Six-Guns and Saddle Leather: A Bibliography of Books and Pamphlets on Western Outlaws and Gunmen* (Norman, 1954)

*The Rampaging Herd: A Bibliography of Books and Pamphlets on Men and Events in the Cattle Industry* (Norman, 1959)

*A Fitting Death for Billy the Kid* (Norman, 1960)

*The Old-Time Cowhand* (New York, 1961)

*Burs Under the Saddle: A Second Look at Books and Histories of the West* (Norman, 1964)

*From the Pecos to the Powder: A Cowboy's Autobiography* (Norman, 1965)

*The Legendary West* (Dallas, 1965)

*The Cowman and His Philosophy* (Austin, 1967)

*The Cowboy and His Humor* (Austin, 1968)

*Western Words: A Dictionary of the American West* (revised and greatly enlarged) (Norman, 1968)

*The Cowman and His Code of Ethics* (Austin, 1969)

*Six-Guns and Saddle Leather: A Bibliography of Books and Pamphlets on Western Outlaws and Gunmen* (revised and greatly enlarged) (Norman, 1969)

*Wayne Gard, Historian of the West* (Austin, 1970)

*The Horse Wrangler and His Remuda* (Austin, 1971)

# The Cowman Says It Salty

# The Cowboy and His Lingo

ALWAYS IN THE PRESENCE of new features of life and divorced as he was obliged to be from older tradition, in speech, as in other activities, the early-day cowman broke through the restraint imposed by established usage and devised a language of his own just as he adopted the strange dress of his calling. The spirit of a creative activity which brought under human control the natural resources of a new country served also to stimulate activity in the creation of fresh word and phrase.

There is always one thing about a man that stamps him for what he is — one thing that is harder to change than all the rest — and that is his speech, for language is as close to a man as his blood. The basic reason for the difference between the cowboy and other men rests on an individual liberty, a lawlessness, an acceptance of his own standards alone. Never having had a chance to "study the higher branches of information through book learnin'," the native cowman forged his own language. Being epigrammatic, this lack of education and his limited vocabulary, together with his terseness, developed him into a painter of word pictures. Mental images were a part of his life and I do not think he has an equal for aptness in his figures of speech.

A combination of conditions has perhaps produced this talent for word pictures. Loneliness, lack of education, and a certain restrained lawlessness all have had their influence. His general impatience of rule and restraint, his democratic enmity to all authority, his extravagant and often grotesque humor, his extraordinary capacity for metaphor — these are indicative of the spirit of the West, and from such qualities its language is nourished.

It is a phase of this same lawlessness, this same reliance on one's self, that makes for his taciturnity and watchfulness. His language, seasoned as it is with Mexicanisms and metaphors peculiar to the range, is as much a part of his lore as life itself.

More than any other avocation of mankind, the pastoral life and industry have enriched modern language with metaphors and similes of striking beauty, concrete significance, and charming simplicity. These two figures of similarity are available as means of renewing the vitality of living speech, but their fossil forms enter largely into the composition of the formal state of the language. By means of metaphor we express more vividly and strikingly our feeling on any subject.

In the coinage of his words, the cowboy exhibits a marked tendency to achieve short cuts in speech by a process of agglutination, and his compounds have been largely responsible for giving his language its characteristic tang and color. His habit of reducing complex concepts to the starkest abbreviations has enormously enriched his language with apt and colloquial metaphors.

He has a talent for stripping language to the bone, taking the verbiage out of an expression and squeezing the juice from it. He is laconic of speech, using few words to express himself, but his meanings are forceful and easily understood by his comrades. He is a creative genius in communicating in a language rich in vigorous similes and anecdote, and like most growths that have real vitality, these figures are deeply rooted in the subsoil of his speech, and are capable of rank and primitive forms.

Does not the expression "sloshed on his hat" picture in four words a man putting on his head-gear in a careless manner better than it could be told in a paragraph? Who but a cowboy would express the act of a man blowing the dust from his hat with such a phrase as "he whistles on it with his breath"? While the ordinary man might express the sudden appearance of a horseman in the road ahead in various inadequate forms, the cowboy pictured it completely by creating a verb in a new sense and said, "he *bulged* into the road ahead," thus depicting in one word suddenness in the strongest possible term. Again, "they came skally-hootin' into town" paints a complete picture of men riding recklessly down the dusty street and drawing their sweating horses to a slithering halt before the hitch rack.

Like other men of the soil, the cowboy's speech seems salty and unrefined, but it sparkles with stimulating vigor. Though uneducated, he never lacked for expression. Perhaps there is a pungency and directness about his speech that seems novel and strange to conventional people, but no one can accuse him of being boresome. His comparisons are not only humorous, but fruited and unfaded. Even with his lack of education, when among men of higher advantages, he is unconscious of this lack because he possesses absolute self-poise and sufficiency.

The more limited and impoverished a person's vocabulary, the greater, as a rule, is his dependence upon slang as a medium of expression. This is true of the cowboy. The early followers of this vocation had little opportunity for schooling and hence resorted to slang for the expression of their thoughts. They have left behind a rich mine of vivid expressions that will be used as long as men handle cattle. The examples of his striking metaphor in slang are legion. No metaphor is too remote for him, no allusion too subtle.

The vividness of his speech manifests itself quite as often in the selection of the apt word as in the construction of his phrases. His peculiar directness of phrase meant freedom from restraint, either of society or convention.

Slang, since the foundation of the United States, has been the natural expression of youth, and the cowboy, whatever his years, is at heart always a youth. Many of his terms, however, though slangy in origin, are not intended to be slang in usage, and they function seriously as an integral part of the West's legitimate English.

I have never yet met a cowman whose speech did not contain a vigorous freshness. He needed no education in his profession. Many of them, as one said, "didn't get past the flyleaf of the primer." Although he held "book learnin'" to be a great thing for the "other feller," he had little use for language "so polished you could skate on it." The man who used words that "showed up as big as a skinned hoss" held his respect, but he much preferred to talk with someone who "didn't stray over in the tall grass with his highfalutin' language," and could "chew it finer" so that he could understand his meaning.

In studying his speech, I think each new acquaintance offers a fresh experience, an untouched pocket of "paydirt" to be mined. The lingo of the cow country has never ceased to fascinate me with its delightful pithiness. On the surface his talk seems crude, but living close to nature as he does, he draws the rough, rich imagery of his incomparable figures of speech from the things he experiences. A word serves to convey meaning often carried by a sentence. To one unaccustomed to his language the cowboy seems violent, but there is nothing more appealing than the jargon of the cowhand when he is among his own kind. Like the man, his language is always vigorous and alive. Most people think him vulgar because he is profane, but he is no more particular about his language or choice of subjects than other classes of men who live with little or no association with women.

His language takes on somewhat the character of the land. Being both courageous and resourceful, he can best express his thoughts with comparisons and exaggeration. He has developed a vernacular partaking of his occupation and full of allusions to the familiar things in his life.

In the early days many men with college degrees came West, fell in love with the freedom of range life, and remained. Unbound by conventions, they were not long in "chuckin'" their college grammar and drifting into the infectious parlance of the cow country. I have never yet met a cowman who did not use it naturally and unconsciously, be he educated or otherwise.

Unlettered folk seem fond of making comparisons to natural objects to express their ideas and feelings. Vividness and freshness are qualities always present. They live close to reality and their talk is pungent and filled with figures and conceits. The hazards of the cowman's life have developed a roughness in his character and put force into his language. Even his play has a rowdiness which makes him, as one old-timer said, "a reckless, don't-give-a-damn fool that's forgot there's such a thing as consequences."

His diction is rich with his own coinages, colored with native slang and variegated now and then by the influence of the Mexican tongue.

With an active mind and in a well-nigh bookless country, he has had to derive his intellectual diversion in part from applied logic, rather than from reading. The cowboy is not hurried and can take the time to examine small things. He looks them over from every side, chews on them and squeezes out all the significant details and adds their essence to his philosophy. His language is full of strange, exaggerated, peculiar illustrations, comparisons, and similes, and his rich choice of synonyms embodies a latent chapter of life and habits. His words, phrases and customs have become community property, his dialect a language of his own, characterized by its simplicity, strength and directness. Unsleeping need for quick thinking and doing have given these nomads the pith of utterance.

Within the cowman's figures of speech, too, lies the rich field of his subtle humor and strength — unique, original, full-flavored. He has moulded language to suit his own needs and is a genius at making a verb out of anything. He respects neither the dictionary nor usage, but employs his words in the manner that best suits him and arranges them in the sequence that best expresses his ideas, untrammeled by tradition. Ordinary words and phrases, freshened to novelty by the cowboy's wit, show his unpremeditated art of brevity, varying in aptness, but in imagination constant. His figures of speech are so sudden they lash out at you like the crack of a whip; so unexpected they are breath taking. His words are refreshing because they have not lost their power and become greasy with usage. His apt, condensed expressions — words still damp with creativeness — tell us so much in so few words, and bring most vivid pictures to mind. When a tenderfoot hears this range vernacular — distinctive, picturesque and pungent — he is "surprised as a dog with his first porcupine." After he recovers from the shock of such unconventional English, the more he listens the more refreshing it becomes, because, "like a fifth ace in a poker deck, it is so unexpected."

The cowboy is usually soft-spoken and reserved in manner with strangers, so much so that he has gained the reputation for being taciturn and reticent by nature, a conclusion which is erroneous. This reserve fell away in the association with each other, and, when a number of them gathered together, they were boisterous enough, and in their stories, sallies and railleries there was much coarseness of language. He did not "loosen up" until among his own kind, and then he could talk aimlessly and volubly, finding plenty to keep the conversation from lagging. Yet he was never a garrulous person. He devised a vocabulary of his own, and developed to a remarkable degree the faculty of expressing himself in a terse, crisp, clear-cut language of the range. When he spoke his hearers had no reason for misunderstanding his meaning, so apt were his slang and figures of speech. It is true that the cowboy who was "mouthy" was not usually held in high repute in a cow-camp, but "mouthy" in this respect referred to a man who could talk of nothing of interest or value, but "just run off at the mouth to hear his head rattle."

Cowboys, because they often had to stay alone for long periods of time when they were outriding, or were posted at a line-camp, were more apt than other men, especially city men, to get out of the habit of talking. Therefore, when they did get with companions they were likely to talk freely to catch up. It was not an uncommon thing for a visitor who rode up to a line-camp or ranch where a lone cowhand was "holdin' it down" to be invited and implored to "get down and stay all night" that the host might be relieved of the monotony of loneliness. When a man who had been for days, and often for weeks, outside the sound of a human voice, came in contact with one of his race, he usually had a great deal of talking to do. Yet when a cowboy met a strange hand on the trail, as a rule he did not talk much until each found out what kind of man the other was. With men not of their calling they were still more reserved.

One of the inherent characteristics of the cowboy is exaggeration. Not only does he have a talent for telling tall tales, but he has a genius for exaggeration in ordinary conversation. An ordinary man, in describing a drunken man, would be content to state that he was "so drunk he couldn't hit the ground with his hat." But the cowboy is never satisfied with ordinary statements. He seeks more strength and adds more words to gain this potency by saying "he was so drunk he couldn't hit the ground with his hat *in three throws.*" Where the ordinary man might say someone "raised hell," the cowboy would say he "raised hell *and put a chunk under it.*" The ordinary man might describe a man tired from running by stating "his tongue was hanging out a foot," but the cowboy would get exaggerated strength by saying "his tongue was hangin' out a foot *and forty inches.*"

By nature the cowboy was not demonstrative, and his setting did not tend to make him so. True, he was gifted with humor of imagination which was oddly introduced into his language and found vent in his justly celebrated story-book slang. Yet in addition to the question of origin, transmission and consequent variations in his speech, the student of language will find in his words a lot of material worthy of attention. He represents a type. The expression of his emotions is interesting, even if he does not employ the usual methods of giving it vent. The real charm, it is true, lies in his direct simplicity. In him we come very close to the primal man. He talks of things that affect his daily life. He develops his own rules of grammar; he employs words in unusual meanings; he borrows from the Spanish *vaquero,* then corrupts the terms to suit himself; often he coins his own words; he creates a vernacular that is so apt and telling that some of his words have found lodgement in the conservative East, and are now found in the best dictionaries.

A pronounced trait of the cowboy is the pithy, yet robust humor which continually crops up in his speech. Humorous intent is back of many of his metaphorical shifts. His is a dry rather than a gay humor. So with his keen sense of humor that takes unexpected slants, and his avoidance of unnecessary words, he seems to express himself more freely with a slang which strengthens rather than weakens. His utterances are filled with this slang, as the reader will see in subsequent chapters.

# I Acquire a Hobby

WHEN I WAS A SMALL BOY my father worked in the general offices of the Southern Pacific Railroad at Houston, Texas. Because he loved animals, he built a home far out on the prairie beyond what was then Brunner Addition. He wanted to be where he could have cows, pigs and chickens. He taught me to be kind to animals and I had a couple of sheep, an angora goat for which he made a harness to pull a little wagon, and later he gave me a little roan pony and a saddle to fit.

I spent much of my time riding over the prairie pretending to be a cowboy. At this time there was a minor cattle trail near our home over which small herds of cattle were frequently driven. Invariably the cowboys nooned a short distance away. I did not know where the cattle were from nor where they were going; but, like all small boys, I was fascinated with the scene. I used to ride to their noon camp to get a closer look and remember that they kidded me with such greetings as: "Hey, boss, here's that bronc peeler you been lookin' for." Or someone would say, "Light, Kid, and cool your saddle," or another might say, "Hop down, cowboy, and line your flue with some whistleberries." I learned early that the cowboy's speech was full of striking metaphors and similes.

I failed to understand this strange language, but it fascinated me and made a lasting impression upon my young mind. Also stamped indelibly upon my memory is one day when a steer got "on the prod" and disembowled a rider's horse. The scene of this cowboy leading his horse into the woods past our home to destroy him is one I will never forget. There was a time, too, when a longhorn steer became lodged between my father's water cistern and the back porch and the cowboys had a hard time getting him out. The language they used made my mother flee into the house, but I was charmed by these strange phrases. Through all these early impressions I became interested in cattle and cowboys as well as their language.

Some years later, after I had grown wise to the realization of what a gold mine recording this language could be, I bought some notebooks in which to preserve the things I heard. I think the serious beginning of my real interest was when a group of cowboys, into which I had stuck my inquisitive young ears, were reminiscing. Jim Houston, a typical Texas cowboy of the old school, was telling of a time he was afoot in a branding pen when a cow got "on the peck."

"There wasn't no love-light in that cow's eyes as she makes for me," said Jim. "I fogs it across the corral like I'm goin' to a dance, and she's a-scratchin' the grease off my pants at ever' jump. Seein' I can't make the fence in time, Brazos Gowdy jumps down off the fence and throws his hat in the old gal's face. Seein' a cowboy come apart in pieces like that makes her hesitate till I climbs the fence without losin' anything more'n some confidence, a lot of wind and a little dignity. You can take it from me, a cow with a fresh-branded calf might be a mother, *but she shore ain't no lady.*"

Such language, aside from its length, is typical of the cowboy. I have told this story in some of my other books, but think it well to repeat it here because it is the real reason for the start of my notebooks. Everyone who knows me knows that collecting the cowboy's language has become my hobby. A man cannot follow a hobby for nearly seventy years without convincing his friends he is a little "loco" on the subject.

We Americans have many varying hobbies and should be encouraged in them. A hobby is a safety valve. Without one we are apt to get into a rut, and to me a rut is a grave with both ends knocked out. Many people think my hobby a strange one. They can understand a man collecting some tangible object like stamps, coins, guns or books. But collecting the speech of a vocation is something hard for them to comprehend, yet it has been a wonderfully interesting hobby. I have gotten much pleasure from it. It has taken me places to meet many interesting people, among them salty old cowhands as well as writers of note. It has caused me to write several books upon the subject and receive some honors I would have otherwise never received.

While in college I chummed with a number of ranch boys from West Texas and from them gathered much material for my notebooks. Throughout my adult years I have visited ranches, attended cattlemen's association meetings, old trail drivers' conventions, the annual Cowboy's Reunion at Stamford, Texas, as well as visiting the stockyards in Fort Worth while living there.

In 1931 I attended the unveiling of a monument at Doan's Crossing near Vernon, Texas, where I had such old-time cowmen as Jack Potter, Ab Blocker and George Saunders, as well as J. Frank Dobie, in my room to talk their lingo while I took notes. During my travels I always stopped at hotels where cattlemen and cowboys loafed in the lobby; such as the Amarillo Hotel, Amarillo, Texas; the Santa Rita, Tucson, Arizona; the Adams Hotel, Phoenix, Arizona; the Rainbow Hotel, Great Falls, Montana; the Plains Hotel, Cheyenne, Wyoming; the hotels of Las Vegas, New Mexico; Laramie, Wyoming; Denver, Colorado, and others scattered throughout the West.

One would think these to be poor places to gather such things, but if he sits with a notebook in his hand as though he were figuring up his expense account and just listens, it is surprising the gems he can capture. As a class, cowboys are rather shy around strangers and it is hard to get them to talk until they get well acquainted with you, but if you sit quietly near a group of them as though they were far from your mind and just listen it will be well worth your while; that is, if you are interested in this endeavor.

One day many years ago I was sitting in the lobby of the Amarillo Hotel and a couple of old cowmen were standing behind me talking of the dry weather. It seems both of them were from New Mexico, where there had been a drouth, and one said, "Out in my section the grass is as scarce as bird dung in a cookoo clock," and the other answered, "It's so dry on my place the bushes follow the dogs around." In the lobby of the Santa Rita Hotel I heard one cowboy describe a little Jewish merchant with, "He's one of them fellers that couldn't say 'hell' with his hands tied."

One night I stood watching a cowboy shaking dice at the cigar counter of the Plains Hotel in Cheyenne. Thinking to compliment the girl behind the counter, he said: "You look as prim as a preacher's wife at a prayer meetin' tonight." One year when I was doing research in the State Library at the Capitol building in Phoenix, I spent my days in the library and my nights in the lobby of the Adams Hotel, occasionally wandering into the bar where the cowboys were gathered. One of them was telling another about a prairie fire he had helped fight and ended by saying, "After that fire the whole country looked like hell with the folks moved out." At another time I heard one say, "I came out here because it's a country where a man can switch his tail."

In the end I was really surprised at the number of examples of the cowboy's lingo I succeeded in picking up around hotel lobbies, but they were numerous. In the earlier days one would not have found this to be true because cowboys did not go to town often, and then only to the saloons. If they stayed all night in town, chances are they would have slept in the livery barn with their horses. As you might know, not all of my collection has been gathered at such places, for I have attended all kinds of meetings and visited many ranches and chuck wagons of the working cowhand in his own habitat.

In the lobby of a hotel in Laramie, Wyoming, one old-timer asked another how his son was getting along, and he answered, "He's gettin' as wild as a corncrib rat." The other acknowledged that his own son was "always flappin' his chaps at some rodeo." I heard two cowmen talking in the lobby of the Rainbow Hotel in Great Falls. I missed the first part of their conversation, but heard one of them end by saying, "I'd as soon teach a bull calf to drink from a bucket." Another, telling what a poor shot a certain friend was, said, "He couldn't hit a bull's ass with a banjo." One year many years ago I was in Las Vegas, New Mexico, to attend the annual rodeo and was sitting near two old-timers — one a former sheriff — when I heard him tell his friend about a certain party whom he said "had been out of Texas long 'nough to tell his right name."

An old cowman with whom I talked in Amarillo, said, "At one time I wanted to settle down and buy me a little spread so I could lie to the tax collector and sanitary man like any cowman. I tried to borrow some money at the bank, but they wouldn't loan me a nickel unless I got the Lord and all His Disciples to go on my note. I reckon that's what first got my hoofs itchin' to see how folks on other ranges lived." I heard another telling his companion about the time there was some shooting in a saloon causing a scattering of men. "They came pilin' out of that saloon," he said, "like red ants out of a burnin' log."

I used to wonder why the cowboy could never seem to resist using some figure of speech when a plain statement would serve his purpose. But during the years I learned that he takes delight in painting these word pictures because it gives his speech that strength for which he strives. I made a return visit to a ranch after several years absence and missed one of the boys for whom I had developed a liking. When I inquired about him, one of the hands, instead of merely telling me he had taken a job as a deputy sheriff, said, "Oh, he's packin' a six-gun for the county, and sportin' a tin badge on his brisket that shows up like a patent medicine sign."

There is an underlying humor in nearly every utterance of the cowboy. Sitting around listening to a group of them talk among themselves is better than the best vaudeville show I ever saw. Their humor is rich and unaffected.

Most of them are full of humorous sarcasm toward another who had failed in an undertaking. He never got sympathy. When a roper missed his throw at a steer for the third time, another cowhand rode over and remarked,

"Say, why don't you put a stamp on it and send it to him by mail?"

A cowboy was thrown from the bronc he was trying to break and he had hardly hit the ground before one of his companions rushed to where he lay and lifted one foot to look at his boot sole.

"What you lookin' for? It's my head that hurts," he said.

"You got throwed so high I was tryin' to see if St. Peter had whittled his initials on your boots," answered the other.

The cowman is very direct in some of his statements. To the uninitiated it would sound like a riddle, but it was no "boggy crossin'" to another cowman.

For instance, one was telling me about his bunkie coming home drunk.

"And you know," he said, "that son-of-a-gun piled into bed just like a rooster."

Not being sure if he meant merely "cock-eyed" and full of "Old Crow," I asked: "How's that?"

"With his spurs on," he answered as if astonished I did not comprehend his meaning without question.

From his association with horses the cowboy's language became somewhat "horsey." For instance, the cowboy goes to the barbershop "to have his mane roached"; he goes to the dentist, or "jaw-cracker" to "have his bridle teeth fixed"; he speaks of his feet as his "hoofs"; his sides as his "flanks"; his chest as his "brisket"; and he speaks of a young girl as a "filly" and her ankles as her "fetlocks."

Like all creators, the cowboy not only built, but borrowed for his own wherever he found it. He borrowed from the Mexican, the French, the Indian, and took what he wanted from the buffalo hunter, the miner, the trapper and the freighter who preceded him, and from the gambler, the gunman and others who came after him. Thus, at the top and bottom of our map, French and Spanish trickled across the frontier, and with English they melted into two separate combinations which are wholly distinct. Some have remained near the spot where they were moulded, while other compounds, having the same northern or southern starting points, have drifted far and wide and become established in the cowpuncher's dialect over the whole country.

From the Spanish the cowboy acquired such words as *adobe* because houses in the Southwest were commonly built of these mud bricks; *adiós,* meaning literally "to God," commonly used in the border cattle country as an expression of friendly leave taking; *cabrón,* the Spanish for "he-goat," a person who consents to the adultery of his wife — and used in the Southwest to mean one of low breeding and principle.

The term *compadre,* meaning "close friend," or "pardner," is frequently used by cowboys on the southern border. The Spanish term *hasta la vista* is also frequently used in the cattle country where Spanish is spoken as a friendly parting equivalent to "I'll see you later."

The word "hoosgow" is now commonly used over the entire country, but it was originally the cowboy's attempt to pronounce the Spanish *jusgado,* meaning "tribunal," or "court of justice." The Spanish *j* is always pronounced like the English *h,* and a *d* between vowels is breathed rather than pronounced. *Junta* is another word the cowboy uses in referring to a business meeting, because in Spanish it means a "congress," "an assembly," or "a council."

The cowboy pronounces the Spanish *quien sabe* "kin savvy." This means "who knows? I don't know," and the cowboy uses it to admit he has no information upon a subject. He has shortened it to "savvy" or "no savvy." He also uses the Spanish *sí* for "yes"; *poco* for "little"; *pronto* for "quickly"; *pueblo* for "town"; *pasear*, meaning to go some place leisurely; and *vamos*, meaning "let's go." He pronounces it "vamoose," and more commonly uses it to mean "get to hell out of here."

He has always reserved control of his spelling and pronunciation, and cares nothing for dictionaries. He pronounces his Spanish as it sounds to his ear, and thus new words have been created. For instance, hackamore has evolved from *jáquima;* and *mañana* is used freely along the Mexican border in association with a leisurely postponement, because the Mexican commonly uses it to mean "tomorrow," or "maybe sometime."

Like all other Americans, the cowboy is in a hurry and employs our typical shortening of words and phrases. His grammar is rough and rugged like his hills and canyons, but his shortcuts are practical. Thus he creates words such as "lariat" from *la reata;* "chaps" from *chaparreras;* and "dally" from *dar vuelta.* Yet in his actions he is not hurried, but takes his time to examine small things. He gets the habit of "usin' his eyes a lot and his mouth mighty little." He squeezes out all the significant items and adds their essence to his refreshing philosophy. As one said, "He has a talent for sayin' a whole lot in a mighty few words," and "don't use up all his kindlin' to get his fire started."

From the French-Canadian he got such words as *cache* from *cacher,* meaning to conceal or hide. This is commonly used by the cowboy, though he inherited it more directly from the trapper. The French-Canadian also furnished the word *parfleche,* meaning the prepared hide of an animal, as of a buffalo hide dried on a frame after the hair had been removed. The cowboy uses this word in speaking of his "poke" or "war-bag" and has changed it to *parflesh.* This word is rarely used in the Southwest except among packers. *Chassed,* from the French *chaser,* meaning "to go," is another term used. "Chassed into" is commonly used as a synonym for "happened upon."

The Indian gave him such terms as "bury the hatchet"; *cultus,* meaning "mean," or "worthless"; "no medicine" and "off the reservation," which the cowboy uses in speaking of anyone speaking or acting out of turn. The Indian word *pow-wow* means a conjuration performed for the cure of disease, attended with noise and confusion, and often with dancing. The cowboy uses the word to refer to a "get-together" for a conference since it, too, is usually accompanied with debate and confusion.

The cowboy also adopted the term "sign language" from the Indian. It is quite a convenient method of communication. The trail boss who had ridden ahead to seek water need not ride all the way back to the herd to give directions. On the horizon he could give signals with his hat which saved him much riding and time.

For something not up to the white man's standard, he uses the Indian word *siwash,* and a "siwash outfit" is the contemptuous name for an unenterprising ranch. Taken from the Indian's custom of smoking the pipe of peace at councils, the cowman uses the term "smoke the peace pipe" when speaking of making up after a quarrel. Founded upon the Indian smoke signals, a method of distant communication, the cowman also uses the term "send up a smoke" as a colloquialism for giving a warning or making a signal.

The Indian word *skookum* means "good," or "great"; and the Northwestern cowboy uses this term as well as "skookum house," which is what his red brother calls the jail on an Indian reservation. The Cayuse Indian jargon for food, *muck-a-muck,* is also sometimes used by the cowboy of the Northwest. The Indian words *teepee, wickiup* and *wigwam* are sometimes used by the cowman in referring to his home or house.

Indirectly, he got such terms as "beef issue," meaning the issue of beef for food for reservation Indians at a government agency. "Fire-water," for whisky, derived from the custom of traders in demonstrating the alcoholic content by throwing a little of the liquid on the fire to let it burn, and "grass money," money paid Indians for grazing rights on Indian land, were frequently used. Also from the Indian custom of scalping his enemy, the cowman got such expressions as "hair lifter," "had his hair raised," "lost his hair," and "lost his topknot."

Many cowboys yearning to see what was "on the other side of the hill," were like a tumbleweed drifting before the wind. They scattered their language until it no longer remained a "boggy crossin'" for a cowman of another section. Yet many expressions remain in the section of their origin. Therefore different sections have their peculiar argot. As Will James said, "The language of the cow country is just as different as the style of the rigs and ways of working."

The Texan says *pitch;* the northern cowboy says *buck;* yet they mean the same thing. Likewise, the Texan's *stake rope* becomes a *picket rope* on the northern range; and *cinch* in the North becomes *girth* when it hits the South. These are but a few examples of many which could be mentioned. California, Oregon, Utah, and Idaho use terms rarely heard in the rest of the cow country.

When Texas first went into the cattle business, it adopted the Mexican's methods and equipment — big-horned saddle, spade bit, rawhide rope, system of "dallying" and all the rest. The massacre at the Alamo stirred in Texas a fierce hatred of all things Mexican and brought changes in following the custom of the Spanish *vaquero.* The long rope and system of "dallying" disappeared, and Texas became a "tie-fast" country. The spade bit was discarded for the grazing bit, and the Spanish rig gave way to the double-rigged saddle.

But the language of the Mexican had deeper roots. This the Texan kept and corrupted to suit his needs. The cattle business of California was also born under Spanish influence, but they had no Alamo, no Goliad. Today it still uses the Spanish rig, the long rope, the spade bit, and the dally. Many other Spanish customs dominate, and the language has been less corrupted.

When the Texan rode over the long trails north, he carried his customs, his speech and his manner of working all the way to the Canadian line. Montana, Wyoming, and other northern and central states adopted much of his Spanish-influenced language. In exchange, the northern cowboy gave the Texan that which he had appropriated from the northern Indian and the French-Canadian, words strange to the man from the Rio Grande.

# When the Cowboy Talks

THERE IS AN OLD SAYING in the West that "there ain't much paw and beller to a cowboy," and the rest of the world has the impression he cannot talk. True, "wide spaces of the plains don't breed chatter-boxes," and "bein' a lone wolf out on the range gets him into the habit of usin' his eyes a lot and his mouth mighty little." Though a stranger might think him "about as talkative as a Piegan Indian," his friends know "he don't depend entirely on the sign language." Though, like the majority of them, he "never had a chance to study the higher branches of information through book learnin'," his companions knew "he could talk so that his conversation don't make a boggy crossin' for another cowman." As one said, "He don't have to fish 'round for no decorated language to make his meanin' clear." If he was talking to an educated man who "spouts words that run eight to the pound," or, as one said, employing "four-legged words that nobody could savvy without an encyclopedia and two dictionaries," he might ask him to "cut the deck a little deeper."

I have heard many expressions to define a talkative man, such as: "He's such a talker he blowed in on his own wind," "his jaw was exercised a-plenty puttin' in a big crop of words," "he could talk a pump into believin' it's a windmill," "he could augur a gopher into climbin' a tree," "he wasn't hogtied when it came to chin music," "his tongue was plumb frolicsome," "he talked till his tongue hung out like a calf rope," "he could talk the hide off a cow," "he had plenty of tongue oil," "they ought to hire him to keep the windmill goin'," "he's as full of verbal lather as a soap peddler," "he's runnin' off at the mouth like a man peddlin' soap," "he's as full of wind as a hoss with the colic," or "he could talk a cow out of her calf."

A person who talked too much might be advised to "hobble your lip," "put a dally on your tongue," "keep a plug in your talk box," "keep your gate shut," "put your jaw in a sling, you're liable to step on it," "button your lip," or "tighten the latigo on that jaw of yours."

A mouthy person might be advised to "save part of your breath for breathin'," or if talking too much while attempting to work, "quit your pantin' and sweat a little"; and one who talked very little might be described with, "He uses his breath for breathin' instead of mixin' it with tongue oil."

After a lonesome ride, when a cowhand met another on the trail, or along a fence line, both would soon swing off their horses and loosen the cinches to give their horses a bit of air. They would then hunker down on their boot heels "in a frog squat," twist a cigarette, and start, as one cowhand said, "fishin' 'round for a cowboy fountain pen, which is a broomweed stalk, and lookin' for plenty of loose dirt to draw in." Another said, "It seems like a cowhand can talk better when he's a-scratchin' in the sand like a hen in a barnyard," for then, with a swipe of the hand, he can have a clean slate and start another lesson in cow geography.

A western "augurin' match," as described by Nyle Kent, "was a case of two loose-tongued jaspers a-settin' cross-legged, knee to knee and face to face, talkin' as fast as they can to see which one can keep it up the longest without runnin' out of words and wind. These two jiggers just jabber at each other like a couple of honkers on a new feed ground."

"At the start," added Don Vestal, "they talk fast and furious, but after an hour or so they slow down to a trot to be savin' of both wind and words. At the end neither of them's got 'nough vocal power left to bend a smoke ring."

Any story a cowhand told "would leave a drummer's yarn kinda faded." When it came to telling tall tales he was a top hand, and in telling these lies "he could make you think Annanias was just an ambitious amateur." As one described such a teller of windies, "He could color up a story redder than a Navajo blanket." Telling these windies was a natural product of the cow country, and it did not take much persuading "to start a puncher on one of those campaigns against truth." It was said of such a man that "he was stretchin' the blanket a-plenty," "he was a good peddler of loads," "he told mighty big lies for such a little man," and "when he finds a listener that ain't alkalied, he piles it on plenty scary." After such a tale told to a group at the chuck wagon, Frank Fowler admitted that "we all knew his saddle was a-slippin'"; and when one hears such a tale, "he lets his ears hang down and listens" because he knows he is being entertained.

When a cowhand felt he was wasting his time trying to give directions or explain something to another who failed to understand, he said he "might as well been talkin' Chinese to a pack-mule." When a group of friends who have not seen each other for some time "start waggin' tongues about the range gossip," it is said "they laugh and joke about this and that till they all run out of smart answers." When men meet on the trail it is time, as one said, "to swap news and saddle-pocket bottles." When a cowboy said of another, "He's one of those medicine tongues that knows it all," he meant that the one spoken of was a fluent talker who thought he was very wise. When one said of another, "I got tired of listenin' to his squaw talk," he meant he had grown tired of listening to irrelevant talk.

The cowman has an unique way of expressing many of his thoughts. If he spoke of one being independent he would say, "He rolls his own hoop"; if he was handicapped someway he "had his leg tied up"; if he complained about something "he kicked like a bay steer"; if he followed someone he "rode into his dust"; and if he was sick or injured he was said to be "ridin' the bed wagon." If he had no knowledge of a subject, he "didn't have any medicine"; if he had gained that knowledge it was said "he's taken a little more hair off the dog"; and if a person was deeply implicated in something he was "bogged to the saddle skirts." An impatient person was said to be "fightin' the bits"; if he gave up on anything it was said that "he surrendered like a willow to the wind." Of anyone trying to put the blame for a certain act upon another, it was said that he was "tryin' to put the saddle on him"; and anyone who had freed himself from some situation had "slipped his hobbles."

An experienced or wise person was said to "set deep in his tree"; a person who hindered another in trying to accomplish something was said to "put a spoke in his wheel"; a confused person "got his spurs tangled up"; a person who was disloyal was said to have "sold his saddle"; a person who bragged too much was said to "throw too much dust"; and when a cowman quit his profession it was said that "he hung his saddle on the fence." If a person was in trouble it was said that he had "got a skunk by the tail." If one was telling what another thought was a lot of "baloney," he was said to be "handin' out a lot of Mexican oats"; and a bully was sometimes described as being "a case of big behavior." On the trail the men who rode drag were said to be "eatin' drag dust"; and when a noisy person was commanded to quiet down he was ordered to "tuck in your shirt-tail."

In dealing with the cowboy's lingo, mention should be made of his profanity. His blasphemy, however appalling it might be, had its foundation on arbitrarily created custom, and not from any wish to be wicked. Many of his expressions, while sacreligious on the tongues of others, were but slang when used by him. The common use of the name of the Deity was with no intention to revile God. All through the West the word "damn" descended from the pinnacle of an oath to the lowly estate of a mere adjective unless circumstances and manner of delivery evidenced a contrary intent. Oaths could be an insult or a term of affection, according to the tone in which they were spoken. Therefore, men were frequently endearingly addressed with seeming curses and apparently scourging epithets.

The cowboy's swearing was, to no small extent, a purely conventional exhibition of a very human and boy-like desire to "blow off steam"; but it became so habitual that, though most cowboys endeavored to refrain from it when in the presence of decent women, few of them were able to "keep the lid on their can of cuss words."

To observe a riot of imagination turned loose with the bridle off, one must hear a burst of anger on the part of one of these men. It would be unprintable, but you would get an entirely new idea of what profanity means. The most obscure, remote and unheard-of conceptions would be dragged forth from earth, heaven and hell, and linked together in a sequence so original, so gaudy and so utterly blasphemous that you would gasp and be stricken with admiration.

The cowboy did not depend upon the commonplace, shopworn terms of the town plodder. It should be said, however, that it was an uncommon thing for him to burst forth with his full powers without fair justification. For this purpose he had a most astonishing vocabulary; and in dealing with a detestable range horse, or in striving to make a half-wild, longhorned, obstinate steer behave himself and go the way he should, nothing but its vigorous employment appeared to fit the circumstances of the case. For use upon such occasions, and also upon sundry others, every well-equipped cowhand of the old times had acquired and kept at his command what appeared to be the entire resources of the Anglo-Saxon speech that could be worked into phrases of denunciation. When he intermingled with them an assortment of picturesque and glowing Spanish expletives and terms of opprobrium, as he frequently did, the earth trembled. Profanity sat naturally and easily upon his tongue, and without it his speech would have been less effectual.

Powerful expletives demand courage and inventiveness. The cowboy possessed both of these qualities. His curses seemed to smoke and sizzle and scorch the atmosphere. They seemed to emit odors, like exploded gunpowder. Sometimes his words were of no known language; he invented them for his own devices, but there was no misunderstanding their meaning. Yet his list of unprintable words did not need to be large, for he was an artist at constantly varying his combinations and putting tonal force into them. Some men devoted considerable thought to the invention of new and ingenious combinations of sacreligious expressions.

To specialized phrases of this sort the admiring public accorded a sort of copyright, so that the inventor was allowed to monopolize for a time both the use of his productions and the praise that they evoked. These individual creations were known as "private cuss-words," and the voicing of such were, under tense conditions, a danger signal or a challenge.

Taken all in all there was an Homeric quality about the cowboy's profanity and vulgarity that pleased rather than repulsed, but which polite society is not quite willing to accept. The broad sky under which he slept; the limitless plains over which he rode; the big, open, free life he lived near to Nature's breast, taught him simplicity and directness. He spoke out plainly the impulses of his heart.

He used profanity as a healthful exercise, as a tonic for irritated nerves, and was therefore ordinarily in a good humor so that the strength of his "cuss-words" was usually spoiled by a good-sized grin.

The cowboy called cursing "airin' the lungs" because it was his way of letting off steam. As one cowman said, "The average cowhand ain't pickin' any grapes in the Lord's Vineyard, but neither's he tryin' to bust any Commandments when he cusses."

It was a natural part of his language and "he could shore cram plenty of grammar into it." As one cowhand said, "Such ripe language wasn't learned at his mother's knee, but seems to come natural from colthood." He never lacked for "cuss" words, "they just rolled out naturally in a blue smoke with all the frills attached." As one observed, "Cussin' was the only language known to mules, and many a skinner's swearin' got so hot it would've burnt his throat if it hadn't been made of asbestos."

In my notebooks are many different cowboys' descriptions of another's swearing, such as: "His language would make a bullwhacker hang his head in shame"; "he could make a bullwhacker's cussin' sound like a Methodist sermon"; "he called him names that'd peel the hide off a Gila monster"; "he released some cussin' that any skinner would be happy to get a copy of"; "his cussin' could take the frost out of a zero mornin'"; "his cussin' would burn the grass to a cinder for yards around"; "when he jerks off the bridle and turns loose you could smell the sulphur"; "he called him names that wouldn't improve a Sunday School none"; "he let out a string of cuss words that'd warm a bullwhacker's gullet"; and "he called him some mule skinner names."

When the boss was bawling out a certain rider another described it with, "He's tellin' him off in words of double-barreled syllables seasoned with cuss words"; and another cowhand spoke of a similar situation with, "He horned him with all the cuss words he could remember."

In speaking of another's swearing ability one cowboy said that "he knew how to swear in paragraphs and had a regular tune to it." Other comments include: "His talk was half-soled with cuss words"; "when it came to cussin' he don't swallow his tongue"; and "he made the air cloudy with his cuss words." Another described a bunch all trying to swear at once with, "Their cussin' sounded like a mule skinners' convention."

# Singin' To 'Em

BUGEYE LAWSON turned off the radio with an angry snap. We were lounging in the bunkhouse of a modern West Texas ranch during that witching hour after supper when men either become talkative or moody. A well-known cowboy song had been coming over the air. At its sudden cessation several of the boys raised up from their bunks.

"What's the matter, Bugeye? You lost your ear for music?" asked Jim Miner.

"Music!" snorted Bugeye. "Them New Jersey cowboy crooners give me a pain I can't locate with a forked stick. Here this one's singin' 'Git 'Long Little Doggie' like he's singin' about a pup instead of the dough-guts that's done so much to develop my cuss words."

"He did have a good voice though," said one of the music lovers.

"Ought to have some redeeming qualities. I'll bet he's so plumb ignorant he don't know dung from wild honey. Ten to one he don't know which end a cow quits the ground with first," answered Bugeye with finality.

"I'm ridin' with Bugeye," said Spike Hunter. "Judgin' from the singin' of these soda fountain punchers you'd think a real cowhand yodels all the time. You don't hear none of that garglin' on the range."

"Seems like ever' feller that can yodel and claw a *git*-tar," put in another, "dudes himself up in hair and leather and gets himself a job bawlin' in a radio so's he can punish the rest of the world with a noise like he's garglin' his throat with hot mush."

This discussion was music to my ears. During my rambles over the West collecting the thoughts and speech of the cowmen, I had often brought up the subject myself to get the native reaction; and I was always eager to hear the cowhand's unbuttoned opinions.

The chief reason for the cowhand's dislike of the radio and TV singer is that here is a poor imitation of himself. This counterfeit is condemned because he cannot ride a bucking horse nor throw a rope. "Them fellers," said one cowhand, "couldn't cut a lame cow from the shade of a tree." Perhaps, too, there is a little jealousy of the superior musical quality of the radio singer's voice.

In his book, *Pardner of the Wind,* Jack Thorp wrote:

I never did hear a cowboy with a good voice; if he had one to start with, he always lost it bawling at cattle, or sleeping in the open, or telling the judge he didn't steal that horse. Some of the cowboy actors and radio cowboys nowadays, of course, have very beautiful voices.

One cannot help but respect the view of a man who spent fifty years of his life riding the range and who was the original collector of cowboy songs. Jack Thorp published the first book of cowboy songs to be printed back in 1908; and he composed a number of songs himself, the most popular being "Little Joe, the Wrangler." His opinion of cowboy voices has been confirmed on every hand by men with whom I have talked throughout the range country.

One night at the Pot Hook wagon the subject of songs came up for discussion. An elderly man who had been with the outfit "as far back as an Injun could remember" offered this comment:

"A heap of folks," he said, "make the mistake of thinkin' a puncher sings his cows to sleep. He's not tryin' to amuse nobody but himself. In the first place, he don't have no motherly love for them bovines. All he's tryin' to do is keep 'em from jumpin' the bedground and runnin' off a lot of tallow. In the second place, these brutes don't have no ear for music, which is maybe a good thing because the average puncher's voice and the songs he sings ain't soothin'. Mostly he has a voice like a burro with a bad cold, and the noise he calls singin' would drive all the coyotes out of the country."

"I'll admit," added Jesse Bennett, "that mostly the songs he sings are mighty shy on melody and a heap strong on noise; but a man don't have to be a born vocalist to sing when he's alone in the dark if he's got a clear conscience and ain't hidin' out."

"Surely there must be some cowboys with good voices," I said, to keep the subject open.

"Oh, sure," answered the foreman of the outfit, after lighting his cigarette with a half-burned stick from the fire. "Once in a while you'll find a man with a good singin' voice and he'll sure be kept busy 'round the campfire renderin' music, because all punchers are mighty fond of bein' entertained with singin'. In fact, they like to swap songs. They like to learn new ones and teach others the ones they know. No matter how moody a puncher gets, he's easy touched with one of those old range songs. A good singer can sure rake the flanks of your heart with one of those mournful ballads a cowhand loves.

"But mostly it's the other way 'round. Not many cowhands have a good singin' voice. You've heard the expression of someone bein' ugly 'nough to stop a clock. Well, not so many years ago I knew a cowhand whose singin' stopped a freight train." The speaker paused to contemplate the dead end of his cigarette. The group became very quiet, as it always does when a group of cowhands are filled with the expectation of a story.

"We called this singer Sooner because he'd sooner borrow than buy," continued the speaker. "One day in town he's freightin' his crop with likker and when he comes out of the saloon, he leans against a porch post and heaves his chin up like a coyote gettin' ready to howl. Then in a whisky tenor he lifts an E-string voice that sounds like a rusty gate hinge and pours forth his soul in song."

There was a heavy pause. Even the night noises seemed to have ceased. As the foreman proceeded to manufacture a fresh cigarette with tantalizing slowness, the silence seemed interminable.

"What about the freight train?" I asked with tenderfoot ignorance, unable to stand the suspense. The relief of the group around the fire was so obvious I could feel it and immediately knew I had pulled a cork under.

"Well," answered the foreman soberly, "just as Sooner starts his song there's a train of Government freighters comin' down the street on their way to Fort Fetterman. When they heard Sooner's voice ever' teamster within hearin' stops and gets down to look for a dry axle."

After such a "sell" there was much boyish whooping

and back slapping, all of which helps persuade the victim that he has become a wiser if not an older man.

On every range I have visited I have heard derogatory remarks concerning the cowboy's singing. One cowhand in Arizona denounced another's vocal efforts as "soundin' like a long-drawn squeak of a slow-runnin' windmill cryin' for oil." The other promptly countered with, "Your voice don't sound like no Christmas chime. The first time I heard you try to sing I thought it was a scrub bull in a canebrake in cocklebur season." One cowboy, in speaking of another's singing, said that "his singin' made you forget all your other troubles. You don't notice trifles when a calamity like the sounds he lets out hits you full in the face."

On another occasion a singer was accused of "singin' in a kiyote key that sounds like you're garglin' your throat with axle grease."

When a cowhand opens his mouth to sing, some kind of noise is sure to come out. What he lacks in musical ability he makes up in lung power. When I was a young man I knew a preacher who could sing louder than the entire congregation put together, but he sang so far off key it made one's flesh crawl. On the Cross N Ranch I met a cowboy with just such a voice. Even in conversation his voice "sounded like an iron tire on frozen snow."

"You call that singin'?" he was asked one day. "Sounds like you're sufferin' with the death rattles."

Other critical opinions of a singer's voice I have heard include: "He had a voice like a burro with a bad cold," "he had a voice as frosty as a November night," or "his singin' sounded like somebody forgot to grease the wagon."

In the early days the long and lonesome job of night herding caused the puncher to sing at his work, both to stay awake and to keep him from becoming as "lonesome as a preacher on pay night." Most of his singing was done when no one was around. Many cowhands who could not be persuaded to sing in company, no matter what the inducement, sang for their own amusement in the middle of a lone prairie.

When the cattle industry was young, it did not take the cowman long to discover that the human voice gave cattle confidence and kept them from "junin' 'round so restless." The practice of singing became so common that night herding is now spoken of as "singin' to 'em." In discussing this subject one old range philosopher told me, "Maybe talkin' could be just as effective, for it's the human voice that gives a cow confidence. However, talkin' out loud to yourself never got to be a popular custom because no man wants another to think he's so feather-headed he needs a wet nurse by talkin' to himself by the hour."

Most of the songs the old-timer sang were set to the religious tunes he remembered from the days when he had a mother "ridin' herd" on him. The words he made up and set to these tunes, however, wouldn't do to put into print, or, as one said, "They were full of language that wasn't fit for parlor talk." He called these songs "hymns," but such hymns, as Curly Mason said, "would shorely jar the clergy with a shock they wouldn't get over soon." As Jack Thorp wrote, such a song would be "just some old hymn, like as not — something to kill time and not bad 'nough to make the herd want to get up and run."

In recent years many beautiful songs of the range country have been composed by musically educated men and made popular by radio and television. As yet they cannot be classed as true cowboy songs, though they may take root and in the future assume a place with the older songs. Meanwhile, one hopes they will not be sung so frequently that listeners will tire of them. "Bury Me Not On the Lone Prairie," said Teddy Blue Abbott, "was another great song for a while, but it ended up like a lot of songs on the radio today; they sang it to death. It was a saying on the range that even the horses nickered it and the coyotes howled it; it got so they'd throw you in the creek if you sang it."

Very few people outside the cow country have heard cowboy songs as they are really sung on the range. They have been so changed and expurgated that the original words are in danger of being lost. In circling the herd the night guard has to sing until he is "plumb tired" of it, or, as one said, "till he sings all the nap off the hymns." But these serenades, with the music of creaking saddle leather furnishing a soft accompaniment, drown out other noises and are "mighty soothin' to a spooky longhorn."

It "sets mighty well" with the hands in camp as they drop off to sleep to hear the faint strains of the songs the guards are singing out where they are circling the herd. As long as a cowhand hears this music he knows everything is "hunky-dory," even if the singer "can't pack a tune in a corked jug."

# Slickin' Up

SOME COWBOYS are more apt than others to spend their wages for fancy duds. When such a man, as Charlie Dunn said, "gets all spraddled out in his low-necked clothes, sloshes on his hat at a jack-deuce angle over his off-eye, and goes swallow-forkin to town in his full war-paint, you can just bet these fancy trimmin's ain't the least in his thoughts."

Brick Hancock, in speaking of a friend duded up in his best, declared: "He displayed a splendor that'd make a peacock go into the discard." It was Charlie Russell, the famous cowboy artist, in referring to one of those fancy cow-dogs, who said, "He's loaded down like a Christmas tree with silver conchas and fancy trimmin's, and when the sun hits him he blazes like a big piece of jewelry and you could see him for miles."

One old-timer, in telling of his trip to town with his wife, said, "The missus made me shave, put on a necktie, pull my britches leg out of my boots and stick my shirttail in, but I was too much of a cowman to let her persuade me to button my vest."

Some cowhands, as one said, "might be a ridin' advertisement for a leather shop, but you'd have to be some persuader to get him to shed his cow riggin' for any of that gearin' of the shorthorn."

I remember one puncher who had the courage to ride into camp wearing a necktie. He would have been hurrahed out of camp, but he swore he was wearing it "to keep his feet warm." Another old-timer, in telling of a time he went to a church social with his wife, said, "When she put that tie on me I thought I was tied to a post."

Some cowboys, especially good ropers and top riders, take a lot of pride in the whiteness of their hands and wear gloves to protect them. These white hands advertise them as being above the laborer, but old Stub Robinson used to argue against wearing gloves because "it was cheaper to grow skin than buy it."

Lem Hurley, in discussing the quality of a good boot, once said, "If I can't put my feet into a decent pair of boots, I shore ain't a-goin' to put 'em into an entire cow." It was Scott McMurray who used to brag that his boots "were so fine you could nearly see the wrinkles in my socks." Once when a saddle tramp rode into camp, Dick Peters noticed his worn-out boots. "Them boots," he remarked, "are so frazzled he couldn't strike a match on 'em without burnin' his feet."

A rep from the Lazy W Ranch told a story one night of a range tramp who "didn't have 'nough clothes to dust a fiddle." Other like expressions I have heard are, "He didn't have 'nough clothes to flag a handcar"; or if the one spoken of was pretty ragged he was "ragged as a sheep-herder's britches." Anyone naked was "naked as a brandin' iron," or "naked as a worm."

Ross Santee told a good story about a cowboy who had bought a cheap wool hat from a Jewish merchant, and this cowboy said: "When the rain caught that cheap woolsey it weighed a ton, even if it did leak like a sieve. My head'd been drier in a gunny-sack and I needed more hands to keep that floppy brim from my eyes if I expected to see anything higher'n my saddle horn." Such a description is typical of the range man.

Anyone dressed in his best fancy outfit might be said to be "all feathered out in his glad rags"; "duded up like a bob-wire drummer"; "ragged out in his fancy doodads"; had on "an outfit that was a flashararity"; or "was duded up like a sore wrist." A cowhand who showed unusual pride in the outfit he was wearing might be said to be "cocky as the king of spades"; "puttin' on more dog than a Mexican officer of revenue"; and "struttin' like a turkey gobbler at layin' time." Or, as one said of such a person, "He walked like a man with a new suit of woolen under-wear." Another spoke of one being "as important as a pup with a new collar."

It amuses the cowboy to see some tenderfoot who "looks like he was raised on the Brooklyn Bridge," come West and dude up in the cowman's rigging. Sag Haywood used to say they "looked like a mail-order catalog on foot." Others have said of such a person that "he looked like a dime novel on a spree"; and a later day cowboy described such a person with, "He looked like a Hollywood movie star on the loose." Upon the sight of one such outlandishly dressed pilgrim, Smoky Clay said, "By the looks of him some deck is shore shy a joker."

Pony Teal, in telling of a tenderfoot dressed in hairy

chaps and a cowhide vest, said that "he came to town wearin' so much leather it was sweatin' him down like a tallow candle," and Charlie Nelms described another with, "From the hair he's wearin' you'd think it's cold 'nough to make a polar bear hunt cover, but it's hot as hell with the blower on." Pie Allard, in telling of another wearing a loud vest, said, "He's wearin' a vest that looks like some painter had upset the color pot on it." In telling the boys of his visit to Chicago, where he had gone with a load of cattle, Bullet Davis informed us that "them city cops was decorated with more iron and leather than the nigh-wheeler of a jerk-line string."

In describing a certain cowboy arriving at a dance at the Two Pole Pumpkin Ranch, Bill Shaw said, "He showed up public as a zebra, wearin' a b'iled shirt and smellin' of bear grease and lavender-flavored soap, lookin' as miserable as a razorback hog stroppin' himself on a fencepost."

Looking glasses were scarce on the early-day cattle outfits and most vain cowboys had to admire themselves with what is called "shadow ridin'," that is, admiring the shadow they cast on sunny days. As one cowboy said, "Clouds have no silver linin' for this breed." Peewee Cox described a friend riding in a hand-tooled saddle with "He's ridin' an illustrated saddle with pictures on it," and said this character "spent his time lookin' at his shadow in that brand new saddle."

The California buckaroo "was a top hand at puttin' on the dog," and "went in for a lot of fancy riggin'." But the Texas puncher "wasn't so much for pretty." As one said, "The chances are he was dodgin' some sheriff and avoided sun-reflectin' gadgets like he would a swamp." Yet he had his vanity. There is an old saying on the range that "for a Texas puncher not to be totin' stars on his duds is most as bad as votin' the Republican ticket."

The cowboy held the dress suits of the city society man to be a ridiculous creation. I heard a cowboy describe one to his companions with, "He had on one of them black suits that's got no front and just a little windbreak down the back," and another described one as "wearin' one of them coats with flaps down the back like a damned scissor-tail bird." Other city clothes came in for his criticism too. Matt Reynolds told of a city man "wearin' one of them stiff collars so high you'd have to stand on a box to spit out."

With the hot dusty work he has to do, the cowboy cannot always "be as clean as a new mirror," but he never passes up a chance to take a dip in a water-hole or creek if he is in need of a bath. The first thing he does when he hits town at the end of the trail is, as one said, "to rattle his hocks for a barbershop where he can take a civilized soakin' in hot water with a big woolly towel and plenty of sweet-smellin' soap."

"Yeah," added Tom Stewart, "and after he comes out of that dippin' vat he buys ever'thing the barber's got and his own folks wouldn't know him either by sight or smell." Weary Sneed once remarked that one such puncher "was so clean and brown he looked like he'd been scrubbed with saddle soap."

To protect his face from sun and wind, the cowboy often let his whiskers grow unless he was riding over to see some nester gal or going to a stomp. On these occasions he dug up a dull razor, stropped it on a latigo strap and tried to make a lather with laundry soap and gyp water. But, as Pecos Yates used to say, "makin' lather with them two ingredients is like tryin' to find a hoss thief in Heaven."

Tin-Ear Toliver told of a time he was standing in front of a busted mirror "tryin' to divorce his bristles," but, he said, "I'm mostly dewlappin' and wattlin' myself till I look like I'd had an argument with a catamount and come out second best." In telling of a time the boys of the

V 7 were getting ready to go to a dance over at the Fiddleback Ranch, Buck Walker said that "all this primpin' was shore hard on the soap supply and stock water. There's a lot of face scrapin' before a busted mirror that suddenly got to be plumb popular, but with a stiff beard and a dull razor it takes more'n a lookin' glass to keep from dewlappin' yourself till you look like the U.S. flag." Another cowhand joined in to say that "all the boys were gopherin' through their warbags to drag out their wrinkled, low-necked clothes that they wear on special occasions and hang 'em out on the brush for the wind to take some of the wrinkles out."

"Then," added another, "with their boots fresh greased and their spurs let out to the town hole so they'd sing pretty, they hit the trail." And speaking of spurs, I heard one cowboy describe a fellow puncher wearing drag-rowel spurs in town, by saying, "His spurs made more noise than one of them old knights that had his clothes tailored by a blacksmith."

Out on the range haircuts did not bother the cowhand much, and he just let his hair grow until he went to town. If he did not get in before it started down his back and clogged his ears so he could not hear well, he would get some puncher, or the cook, who was handy with the shears, to "gather his wool crop." In the old days an Indian haircut was the only one of which he was shy. As one cowhand said, "This called for a certain amount of hide, and no puncher wanted to see his hair hangin' from an Injun's belt. Havin' his hairpins undone that way was a shock to his idea of barber work." Along this line another puncher said, "An Injun shore wouldn't take no blue ribbons at barberin', accordin' to the white man's standard."

On getting up in the morning the first thing a cowhand reaches for is his hat. After that come his boots, then the next thing he reaches for is his sack of Bull Durham.

After a few drags on a cigarette he hoofs it over to the wash-basin to snort in it a couple of times to get the sleep out of his eyes. That done he paws over a towel, which, judging from its complexion, "has been plumb popular."

Of course there are times, especially on roundup and at branding, when the cowhand gets "as dirty as a flop-eared hound"; and to an outsider "he looks like he was plumb water-shy," and unpicturesque with "his flag at half-mast," but he would not be a cowboy if his shirt tail were not out half the time.

On the other hand, there are some who are naturally dirty and stay that way from choice. Kip Gunter used to tell of an old cook who worked for the Chain C wagon. "He's always got his jowels full of Climax," said Kip, "and ain't particular where he unloads it. Furthermore, his clothes are so stiff with beef blood and dry dough you'd have to chop 'em off."

One night in the bunkhouse Chub Davis told of one of the boys who had been out to an Indian camp for a week. After his return to the ranch Chub said, "We found him a-settin' on the side of his bunk readin' his shirt by lamp-light," which meant he was searching the seams of his shirt for graybacks. "He's furnishin' bed and board to a whole cavvy of these crawlin' homesteaders," continued Chub, "and I'll bet if he'd a-took off his clothes you could've drove 'em down the road."

"I'd rather have graybacks than fleas anytime," spoke up Fred Meeker, " 'cause them seam squirrels graze and bed down, but a flea ain't never satisfied. After he locates paydirt on one claim he jumps to stake another one, and he's a damned nimble prospector." And while on the subject of dirt, another cowhand told of a dirty nester with, "It was hard to tell which needed dippin' the worst, him or his cattle."

When an old Indian was visiting camp, Chinook

Oatums complained that he "was considerable whiffy on the lee side." And speaking of things smelly, Lafe Mozier said of an old buck-nun's cabin that "it smelled stronger than a wolf's den," and Dave Cramer spoke of such a place where "the stench was so thick in that cabin the candles were ashamed to burn." In describing an old scummy water-hole full of slime and carcasses of dead cattle, another puncher said the place "smelled like hell on house-cleanin' day." After a die-up that followed a drouth in Arizona, Pike Butler said that "the whole valley smelled like a packin' plant before the pure food law." I have heard other expressions on this subject, such as "strong as a sheepherder's socks," and "it smelled like an Apache gut feast."

# Bendin' An Elbow

DURING MY MANY YEARS of collecting the cowman's language as a hobby, my association with the cowboy had largely been confined to ranches and "the wagon" during roundup, with frequent visits to cowmen's conventions and various rodeos.

It was Dusty Lynch, a cowboy of New Mexico, who suggested broader fields. Dusty once said I was "crazy as a parrot eatin' sticky candy" to be spending good time collecting such stuff, and insisted that cowhands talked just like any other plain, everyday humans. For a long time no one could convince him that I wasn't "plumb weak north of the ears," but he finally became interested enough — mostly through curiosity — to suggest that we ride to the little nearby cowtown on payday where I could meet the boys from other ranches who would be "ridin' in to spill a pot of paint."

"If you'll calf 'round any saloon while the boys're gatherin' a talkin' load," he confided, "you'll maybe collect some remarks to put in your little tally book. Ketch 'em before their tongues get so thick they have to resort to the sign language, and you'll hear some real verbal lather. It's the first few cow swallers of that conversation fluid that brings out the tongue oil."

When that anxious day arrived, we and a number of the other hands went out early to "throw leather on our horses" and were soon on our joyous way to "bend an elbow" with the boys.

Upon our arrival in town we found the hitch racks crowded with horses. It looked like every man in the county was there, all suffering from the disease known as "bottle fever."

"We'll lean our hosses in the livery stable," said Dusty. "No man that thinks anything of his hoss will let him fight flies at a snortin' post while he fights booze at a bar."

Pretty good philosophy I thought.

This town was of the typical false-front variety where most of the doors swung both ways. The first place we entered seemed to be the popular saloon of the town. It was crowded and already becoming boisterous with loud-mouthed conversation and the friendly back-slapping of new arrivals. The man in the once-white apron on the "sober side of the bar" was eyeing the crowd with growing apprehension.

"I'm thinkin' you'll soon be hearin' some chin music you can use," said Dusty, as we paused near the door to consider the motley crowd through a stratified layer of tobacco smoke. He then moved forward quickly to slap an old friend on the back with, "Hyah Zeb, you old catawampus. Whatcha doin' here lappin' up likker like a fired cowhand?"

"Thish is barg'in day," answered his friend Zeb Fisher drunkenly. "The old bar-dog here's shervin' a free schnake with ever' drink."

"Yeah," said a fellow next to Zeb, raking his spurs ruthlessly on the once varnished bar front, "this t'rantula juice'd draw blood blisters on a rawhide boot."

"How the hell do they keep such stuff corked?" put in a third drinker. "It'd shore grow horns on a muley cow."

"Oh, I guess it ain't so bad," grinned Dusty. "You fellers are soakin' it up like a dry sponge."

"It's done took the firsh layer off my tonsils," complained Zeb.

About that time a young red-headed puncher started to leave, "reelin' 'round like a pup tryin' to find a soft spot to lie down in" until he could get his sense of direction. When he finally discovered the door and zigzagged toward it, someone yelled, "Hey Red, somebody's done stole your rudder." Then everyone laughed, and I found Dusty's prediction coming true. I had discovered a new fountain-head for many rich examples of the cowboy's lusty speech.

When it comes to drinking, the cowboy, as one said, "don't belong to the garden variety." He does not, as another said, "have an educated thirst that calls for bottles with pretty labels and silver-foiled bonnets on 'em." He seldom wastes his time on wine and fancy mixtures, and has little appetite for beer because in the old days he could seldom get it cold. Whisky was his drink, and he took it straight, occasionally with a small chaser. Like a cowhand accused of being "water shy" — meaning bodily unclean — who promptly answered: "I ain't afraid of water. In fact, I like a little for a chaser once in a while." Usually though, the chaser is ignored because the drinker "don't want to put the fire out."

Right here let me correct the impression left by the early dime novelists that the cowboy "had nothin' to do except wear his boot soles out on a brass rail," or was said to be "whettin' his boot heels off on a brass rail," or "savin' his boot soles by keepin' 'em on a brass rail." These yellow journalists only saw him when he hit town at the other end of months on the trail fighting dust, loneliness, swollen rivers, stampedes, and general bovine cussedness. When the drive was over, he was relieved of any exacting responsibility, and, being young and full of vinegar, he "cut his wolf loose and freighted his crop with likker."

His noisy exuberance was but the expression of a young, free spirit and healthy body. I have seen college students after a victorious football game just as drunk and their backfiring jalopies noisier than the popping of pistols. And who wouldn't rather meet a drunk on a horse than one behind the wheel of an automobile? At least the horse has some sense.

The pulps continue to follow this perverse pattern of making the cowboy a savage in chaps. Yet cards and whisky are strictly forbidden on all well-managed ranches. This ban is not based upon religious principles. Cow work is dangerous even for sober men, and for one befogged with booze it would likely be fatal. Card playing leads to quarrels and hard feelings among men young and reckless, and at best keeps them up late. Since the cowboy is limited in his drinking to his infrequent visits to town, he does not drink as much as the town inhabitant.

Yet fiction persists in filling his life with booze, bullets and badmen and making his existence one round of gambling, guzzling and gore. Pardon my wandering from the trail in his defense, but such misrepresentation of this lovable American character is my pet peeve.

I am glad I have been privileged to mingle with his kind when his "crop was freighted with scamper juice," for then he possesses "more lip than a muley cow" and has added pages to my notebooks.

When a cowhand goes to town to make a night of it, it is said that he "rides in to hear the owl hoot"; "gets on a high lonesome"; "stays out with the dry cattle;" "rides to town to get roostered up"; or to "let his weakness for booze run wild." Jug Jetter acquired his nickname because it was said he "never went to town till his jug needed fillin'."

I have heard the cowboy give many descriptions of his drunken companions, none of them being what you would call elegant, but apt nevertheless. Alkali Upton spoke of one as having a "full-grown case of booze blind"; Hunk Bowden declared that another "never knowed he had a twin brother till he looked in the mirror behind the bar." Another cowboy spoke of one as being "drunk as a hillbilly at a rooster fight." Shanks Malloy spoke of a staggering drunk "knockin' 'round like a blind dog in a meat shop"; Rawhide Pryor referred to a habitual drunkard as a "walkin' whisky vat." "Drunk as a b'iled owl"; "drunk as a fiddler's clerk"; and "drunk as a Mexican opal" are common cowboy expressions.

Some men just take on enough "tonsil varnish" to loosen their tongues. In time they get what the cowman calls "diarrhea of the jawbone," and their prattle "sounds like rain on a tin roof." If you keep them well supplied with small doses of "neck oil," they can run a long time and they have so much to say "it gets in their way." Yet they stay "as peaceful as a church," seemingly content to stand with a hand curled lovingly around a glass and just talk.

Others are primed with "cow swallers" of the "stuff that cures snake bites," and they cannot stop until they get floored or frenzied. One of this breed usually has a "bronc disposition," and by the time his hide is full of "red disturbance" he is also full of peevishness and starts "haulin' hell out of its shuck." In the words of Pieface Bender, "Hell goes on a holiday when he hits town"; and Cal Gross once said of such a man, "He's givin'" the town hell with the hide off." When a man of this type gets drunk he wants everybody to know it, and they usually do if they are in the same county.

The quality of liquor served in some of the frontier saloons could, as one cowboy said, "eat its way to your boot soles." Hoot Gilroy, complaining of such liquor, told the bartender that he "forgot to strain this stuff to get out the tobacco leaves." Muley Metcalf once stated to a barkeep in Tucson that "you should a-been a snake charmer, judgin' from the likker you're shovin' across the mahogany"; and Bill Pitman told another in Cheyenne that he "might be the best bar-dog that ever waved a bar-rag, but I don't want you spittin' tobacco juice in the barrel to make it pleasant to the taste." Charlie Russell once said such whisky was "a brand of booze that a man could get drunk on and be shot through the brain and it wouldn't kill him till he sobered up"; and Speed Carlow claimed emphatically that "you couldn't gargle that brand of hootch without annexin' a few queer animals." Another said, "A few swallers of that liquid fire and you'd be plumb numb and unconscious." I heard another remark that such whisky was "likker that made you see double and feel single."

Joggy Marsh, speaking of a friend who was always "thirsty as a mud hen on a tin roof," said he lost him in town one day and went searching the saloons for him. "I finally found him," said Joggy, "paintin' his nose in the Blue Front, him bein' busier'n a prairie dog after a rain with this accomplishment." Another spoke of a friend going across the street to a saloon with: "He bowlegs it over to his favorite bar to innoculate himself against snake bites"; and still another spoke of a friend with: "I found him hibernatin' in the Acme Saloon where he was bellied up to the bar and had his boot heel on the brass rail like he intended it to take root." Clint Wilson spoke of one drinking as "nosin' his way to the bottom of a glass," and Tuck McLaren once referred to a heavy drinker as "wearin' himself out bendin' his elbow to look up the neck of a bottle." Another spoke of one who "could hold more likker than a gopher hole." Drinking on the trail at night was often spoken of as "taken' a look at the moon through the neck of a bottle."

Other expressions concerning drinking I have heard are such as, "he's usin' his rope arm to h'ist a glass in place of a rope"; "he's filin' away his nosepaint"; and, "he's busy paintin' his tonsils."

Snug Davis, in telling of an occasion when he and a friend rode to town "to see the elephant dance," said, "We went in to paint the town red, but after a little session of poker we just had 'nough left to buy a couple of pots of paint and a mighty small brush." Spike Dodson spoke of a cowhand "eatin' booze till he got to the state where he sees things that ain't there," and Magpie Curry told of another who "got to seein' things that ain't in natural history."

In my wanderings through the cattle country I have heard a few descriptions of walking while drunk which are amusing. Tom Foster spoke of a man "so likkered up he couldn't walk, but was just feelin' 'round." Speed Logan, speaking of a time he was pretty drunk himself, said, "My boots wouldn't track, and I felt like my legs were a burden." Another cowhand, speaking of an old drunken horse trader in town, said, "The way he's spraddlin' down the street you'd think walkin' was a lost art." Usually when a group of cowboys hit town after a long session of hard work at the ranch, they "didn't lose no time in puttin' on the rollers," and "the saloons and poker joints all got plumb fat and prosperous as soon as they hit town." Some of them "couldn't quit no mor'n a loser in a poker game." It was not long until "his breath would crack a mirror."

The cowman has little use for a prohibitionist. Even if he does not drink himself, he feels it to be unjust to legislate away another man's privilege. It is said on the range that a prohibitionist will "take anything that ain't nailed down except a drink." A man might stay as "sober as a muley cow," or keep "sober as a watched Puritan," and still not vote for prohibition. Kansas Joe, a puncher on the old Fiddleback, said that in his home state "nobody drank likker without hidin' out in the cellar," but that "they could drink more in one swaller than the average man could in an hour because they were in the habit of making one drink go as far as it could before they had to hide out again." Clee Taggart, speaking of a drunkard during prohibition days, said, "He drank so much hair oil he had to eat moth balls to keep down the fur."

A "night out with the dry cattle" might "take all the tallow" out of a man's bankroll and keep the bartender as "busy as a beaver makin' a new dam," but the next morning brought remorse, misery and not a few salty descriptions of his feelings.

Colorado Benson described his feelings by saying, "The next mornin' I had a head so big I couldn't crowd it into a corral." Tucson Williams admitted that "next mornin' I felt like the frazzled end of a misspent life." Center-Fire Mahan once said, "Next mornin' I had a taste in my mouth like I'd had supper with a coyote. If I'd a-had store teeth, I'd taken 'em out and buried 'em." Another "shore had a brindle taste in his mouth," and Milt Scruggs once said, on a morning he had had plenty the night before, "After wakin' up with a head big 'nough to eat hay with the hosses, I reckoned the drouth was over." Years later I heard another declare, "I had a dark-brown taste in my disposition and an oversized head." After one of those all night sessions, Cactus Price declared, "I'm so shaky I couldn't pour a drink of whisky into a barrel with the head out." Nevertheless, if he had any money left he would slip a bottle in his saddle pocket so there would be some "hair off the dog" on the trail back to the ranch.

Once on my way to visit the Swinging L Ranch I met one of its riders in town who offered to ride with me to show me the way. But first he stopped at one of the saloons and told the bartender to "prepare a quart of Old Crow for travelin'." This "old bird" had not traveled far before its contents began to be lowered considerably. After we had ridden what seemed to me a great distance, I asked him how much farther it was to the ranch. He pulled the bottle from the saddle pocket and held it up to the sun. After giving the line of liquid contents careful consideration, he made the startling reply: "'Bout six drinks down the trail," adding hastily with a grin, "plus an eye-opener if I can get by the Old Man with this bottle."

Usually when a cowhand left town, he went "ridin' out of town with nothin' but a head and some debts"; or, as one said, his "head's mighty heavy and his pockets plenty light."

Many a cowhand had a secret ambition to become a bartender when he became too stove-up to ride the "snuffy ones" any longer. Not because he wanted to see life from the "sober side," or learn the art of "yawnin' on the glasses to give 'em a polish," but because he wanted to remain among his own kind — men who could "talk cow."

In the early days, unless the saloon owner hired a professional bouncer, the barkeep had to be a fighter, keeping near at hand a bung-starter, a blackjack or a six-gun. When he reached for the bottle from which you had been pouring your drinks and hammered the cork home with the heel of his hand, he told you plainer than words that your credit had run out, or that in his opinion you had had enough.

The bartender held a prominent place in many of the cowboy's figures of speech. Such phrases as "busy as a bartender on paynight," "genial as a bartender to a sheriff," and "colder'n a bartender's heart" are examples.

An habitual drunkard, who was always "sloshin' 'round a saloon," was said to "wear callouses on his elbows leanin' on the bar." One cowhand described such a character with, "He's a lazy, worthless cuss, spendin' most of his time calfin' 'round a saloon." A man having a few too many, and "havin' a high heeled time," might be spoken of as "he's lit up like a honky tonk on Saturday night."

When a bartender with his deceiving smile asked you to "name your p'izen," it was just a matter of form and about all he got for an answer was a nod of the head because all he had in stock was rye and bourbon. He had no knowledge of or use for drinks that called for olives or red cherries or fizz water, nor did he waste ice by putting it in drinks to weaken the whisky.

Like the old saying, "A corkscrew never pulled no one out of a hole," there are men who go into a barroom to build up their courage when they are "lookin' for someone." They very often have to prove this courage. There are others who try to drown their sorrow in liquor; but they, as one said, "only irrigate it." As one old-timer said, "Givin' some folks likker's like tryin' to play a harp with a hammer."

# Chips That Pass in the Night

The average old-time cowhand had a strong passion for gambling and was apt to gamble recklessly. Most were young men, footloose, and without responsibilities. While card playing furnished excitement and a fascinating pastime, it was not an obsession with them. Many played to kill time, or to practice for a day when they hoped to get to town and buck the professionals. They might even practice some second dealing, hoping to get even with the slick town dealers.

Very few ranches allowed gambling on the ranch, as it created enemies, took the players away from their duties, and kept them up late at night. But the bosses were not always there to see what was going on, nor did they visit the bunkhouse very often. There might be some gambling going on, too, around a campfire where a saddle blanket would be used for a table. Charlie Russell once said, "You can tell a saddle-blanket gambler's luck by the rig he's ridin'." These games were usually small, and a small-time gambler became known as a "saddle-blanket gambler."

The cowhand's work on the range was hard and dangerous, and the pay small. He could not help but hope that he could beat the game in town and win more in a few hours than he could earn by working for several months. After the cattle were delivered to the shipping point, there was a letdown for the cowhands and they felt free to do as they pleased for a day or so.

When he did get to town it did not take him long to put his money into circulation. After buying a few clothes and replenishing any equipment he needed for his riding rig, he had little further use for money except the "fun" it would buy. To make sure he did not leave town with any of it, the saloons had various gambling games. The gambler knew the lure of the games for the cowboy and had the cards stacked. Against the professional gambler the cowboy, as one said, "didn't have no more show than a stump-tailed bull in flytime."

Joe Veach, telling of his losses in a poker game, claimed that "I lost my money like I had a hole in my pocket as big as a pants leg." One young loser I know "didn't ride home singin' with his tail up" after a session of poker, and Corky Gleason spoke of another whose "pockets sprung a leak, and he went home talkin' to himself like a sheepherder." I saw Dunk Stevens "buckin' the tiger" one night in an Arizona saloon. Later I asked him how he came out, and he answered by saying, "When that game was over I didn't have a tail feather left."

Rowdy McCloud, a friend of mine with a weakness for cards, told me of his "settin' up all night tryin' to find somethin' better than some very young clubs," in a game where the dealer "seemed to know both sides of the cards, the way luck was camped on his shirt tail." His opponents, said Rowdy, "kept showin' me hands that looked as big as a log house, and after that session I could count my coin without takin' it from my pocket." One cowhand spoke of a dealer who "packed a heavy jag of luck," and Spike Hunter expressed the same thought with, "For me there never was 'nough spots on the cards, but that dealer could outhold a warehouse." In telling of losing a pot against a flush, another cowhand said of his opponent, "He showed me a hand of five, all wearin' the same complexion," and Speck Devine, speaking of a game which got his roll, said, "Before that game was over, I wished I had all the change them bartenders forgot to give me back."

Chub Davis told of a night when he "couldn't beat a drum" because he "never got nothin' higher'n a two-spot." In telling of a game in which two gamblers started seesawing him, Stud Mayfield said his "luck kinda ravelled out, and they cleaned me down to my spurs." In speaking of a poker game which developed into sky-limit, Chet Savage said, "The game started kinda small, but gathered a heap of moss." Upon several occasions I have heard cowboys speak of some acquaintance starting a game with plenty of money, but quitting loser — which was nothing unusual. Rusty Hawkins described such an occasion with, "He started with a roll as big as a wagon hub, but his luck got to runnin' kinda muddy." Bugeye Lawson told of a like incident of his own experience by saying, "When I started, I had plenty of money and six-bits over; when I quit I'd a-settled for the six-bits." Another loser said that when he started the game, "I had 'nough money to be called 'Mister,' but I was jes' called — too many times." When the cowboy gambled with those professionals "he had about as much chance winnin' as a grasshopper that hops into an anthill," but he found all of them anxious to make his acquaintance.

A big winner — usually the house man — was said to

be "wallowin' in velvet"; "had 'nough money to singe a canebrake"; "had 'nough money to burn a wet mule"; "was grass bellied with spot cash"; or, as one said, "He had more money than he could keep dry." When one was broke — usually the cowboy — he "was cinched to the last hole," and when he was flat broke the gamblers "had him down to the blanket."

Another once told a yarn about a friend who felt he had been cheated in one of the cowtown games, and he concluded his remarks by saying, "He comes into camp full of brimstone and tornado juice, figgerin' he'd get his belt full of shells and go back and blast a lot of those tinhorn gamblers all the way into Boot Hill." Marsh Fowler used to say that "if a gambler changes his name once a month and keeps on the move, he's got an even chance of outlivin' a dumb rustler." In one poker game in which it appeared there would be some gunplay, Walter Mansfield said, "I eased my chair back and got ready to slide under the table."

The mendacious advertising of these twin sins — drinking and gambling — of the cowboy has been unjust. Those who know him best know that he neither drinks nor gambles more than men in other walks of life. Perhaps he has attracted more attention because he sins more noisily. I am glad I knew a few who "raised their rope arm to h'ist a glass," or wagered their money and luck against the gambler's knowledge and crookedness, even if they "didn't have a tail feather left" when they quit. Their speech on these subjects has greatly enriched American slang. I have found them quicker of tongue than of the trigger. Their genius for rich inventiveness created words and phrases wet with novelty, speech I hope I never become stupid enough to resist.

# Ketch My Saddle!

KETCH MY SADDLE! This urgent plea is sure to be yelled on the range when a rider has been thrown and the horse is running away with his saddle. He cares nothing for the horse — it belongs to the company, but the saddle is his own private and highly prized property. Such an event is also called "carryin' the news to Mary."

I remember hearing the call, "Ketch my saddle!" shouted one frosty morning many years ago at the start of a spring roundup on a West Texas ranch. To emphasize the urgency of his plea, Calamity Thompson was wildly jumping up and down, as one cowboy said, "like an empty barrel boundin' downhill." Calamity was not alone in losing his saddle. Other members of the crew, stiff from an inactive winter, were trying to "iron out the humps and kick the frost out" of mounts "snuffy" from the long rest and the animal joy of spring. They were being thrown in all directions. As one cowhand later described it, they were "fallin' off like wormy apples in a high wind."

A cowman will "talk hoss" as long as he can find anyone willing to listen. This is the thing nearest his heart. And since riding is the daily life of his profession, his conversation is filled with his riding experiences and others' ability, or lack of it.

The cutting horse is the pride of his life. One will claim his top cutter "can turn on a button and never scratch it," while another brags that his whittler "can turn on a biscuit and never bust the crust." Matt Rogers once made the statement that his cutter "could turn through the eye of a needle," and another said, "That bay in my string can cut a gopher from his hole." Jud Cramer said his cutting horse "was so good he could cut fly specks from a can of black pepper," and another bragged that his horse "could turn on a quarter and leave 'nough change to buy a bottle of beer." In describing a cutting horse cutting a calf from the herd, one cowhand said, "This hoss stuck to that calf like a bur to a sheep's tail."

Dobe Miller, in telling of shoeing a green bronc, said, "I tacked iron on ever'thing that flew past." Flash Hardy told of a horse that he claimed "was so gentle you could stake him to a hairpin"; and Buzz Carson, referring to an old plug he had seen an aged Mexican riding, said, "That old hoss he's ridin' was dead, but just wouldn't lay down."

In telling of a long, fast ride he had to make, Josh Sanderson said, "After that ride my hoss was covered with lather like some barber had prepared him for a shave." The cowboy's description of a rider rushing up to a hitch rack in town and bringing his horse to a sudden stop would likely be couched in such language as "he fogs up to the snortin' post and spikes his hoss's tail." In discussing various horses, I asked a cowboy on the T Cross 6 about the cowhand's favorite horse other than his cutting horse.

"That would be his Sunday hoss," he answered. "As a rule this hoss was a fancy, highsteppin', all 'round saddler, but for cow work not worth a damn — except to ride down the road."

The roughstring rider had to be good, even better than the man who just broke horses, and a good one was hard to find. The best cowhands could ride the snuffy ones, but wouldn't. This was the buster's job, and he got a few dollars more a month than the average hand. The buster's job was spoken of as "bustin'," "gentlin'," "snappin' broncs," or "twistin' out." A top twister wouldn't give a dime for a bronc that didn't buck and show some spirit when ridden. Yet, if he was a good one he had to have patience and take plenty of time, especially if he was breaking young horses. It was the contract buster who was "bustin' " them at so much per head that hurried them along by rough methods. This is one reason ranchers who wanted good cow horses put their busters on the regular payroll.

As a rule the tall, wiry-framed cowhand could stand the riding game better than the heavy man. A man following this pursuit had to be reckless, daring, and know how to laugh when things seemed bad. When he got old enough to quit enjoying the game and started being careful and serious, he had better tell the boss to give him regular cowboy wages and a gentle horse to ride. Then when he heard that fearful bawl of a bad bronc, he could enjoy it because the other fellow was riding him. Every cow outfit had its roughstring. It was made up of broncs, young horses, and old outlaws or spoiled horses that the average cowhand couldn't or wouldn't ride.

Bronc riding was mostly for young men, and they

were too old for the game at thirty, all crippled and busted up inside. Then they had to have some younger man do their breaking and were satisfied to ride the gentle ones. Breaking horses on a ranch was very different from riding one out of a chute for ten seconds with a pick-up man there to get him as soon as the whistle blew. At the ranch he tried to keep the horse from bucking, but at the rodeo he wanted him to buck his best so he could show his riding ability and win a championship. Riding bucking horses at the ranch was not for show unless the buster wanted to put on a little one of his own. Mostly it was strictly business, and the rider was trying to build his reputation as a gentler of wild horses.

During my wide wanderings over the cow country gathering idioms and picturesque expressions of the cowman, many pages of my notebooks have been filled with his speech concerning horses and his riding of them.

I once asked a roughstring rider on a horse ranch what special qualifications were needed to make a good buster. He scratched his head in thought for a moment, then answered seriously, "You got to have a strong back and a weak mind — to be heavy in the seat and light in the head. Above all you have to keep one leg on each side and your mind in the middle, and every bronc stomper is old at thirty."

"You hear folks talk about breakin' a hoss," said Clate Emory, top rider of the Mill Iron Ranch. "A real rider don't break nothin except maybe an arm or a leg once in a while. We just try to gentle the bronc so some other rider can stay on him. Of course there's some bronc fighters that ain't worth their salt who slam a hoss 'round till they break his spirit, and a hoss with a broken spirit's as worthless as a four-card flush. The boss wants cow hosses, not spoiled hosses, so these riders don't last as long as a drink of whisky on a first-class ranch."

As one buster told me, "Ridin' the roughstring ain't like attendin' a knittin' bee." Breaking horses as a profession is a highly dangerous calling. Bruises, broken boncs, hernia and torn kidneys are the buster's ultimate reward — if he is lucky. The tragedy he most dreads is being "hung up" in a stirrup and dragged to death, or being crushed by a "throw back," the trick of a killer. And more than one rider has been "kicked into a funeral procession." He is forced to retire from the calling in a very short time, young in years but so old in body "he don't travel like a colt no more," and has to be content to ride the gentler horses.

When I asked another bronc snapper why he took up such a dangerous calling, he assured me he didn't "ride the roughstring just for a close-up view of the stars," but for the money there was in it. Quite frequently one will hear some braggart claim he "can scratch hell out of anything that wears hair," but they are all familiar with that old saw, "There ain't no hoss that can't be rode, there ain't no rider that can't be throwed."

"A bronc twister maybe ain't strong on brains," said Spade Taylor, "but he ain't short on guts." When a rider of the bad ones falls in love or gets married he usually quits as a professional. He now has someone dependent upon him and he looks upon life more seriously. How to fall is one of the first things the rider of a bronc must learn. He must know how to kick free from the stirrups, to keep from being dragged by one foot, and to grow limp and hit the ground rolling. A rider always knows he is going a jump or two before he actually goes. He looks for a soft spot to land if possible, taking pains to roll beyond reach of kicking heels and striking forefeet. As one cowhand said, "You have to know how to get off them broncs without 'em stickin' a hoof in your vest pocket." A fall has no terrors for the seasoned rider, for he has had many of them.

It does not mean that a man is a good rider because he works on a ranch. Like the old saying, "There's a heap more to bein' a cowpuncher than just settin' on a hoss and lettin' your feet hang down." And any Westerner knows that "polishin' your pants on saddle leather don't make you a rider." Good riders are born. The rider of the "raw ones" is far above the ordinary hand. His is an exalted position, and he has learned the hard way to appreciate that old adage, "A saddle seat's the easiest thing to find, but the hardest to keep." If he is a good buster he takes great pride in making good cow horses out of his charges, and he never forgets that iron-clad rule, "You've got to control yourself before you can control your horse."

Sooner or later every good rider meets his Waterloo. He is not ashamed of being "grassed" by a good bucker. He holds no grudge, but much admiration for one of those "hard to set" horses.

It is in speaking of being "throwed" that the cowboy is free with his salty language and humorously picturesque descriptions. Hawk Nance, in telling of a time he "met his shadow on the ground," said, "I didn't break nothin', but all the hinges and bolts were loosened." Wash Calhoun told of another rider who "went sailin' off, his hind legs kickin' 'round in the air like a migratin' bullfrog in full flight."

One night on a Wyoming ranch when the conversation had drifted into horse breaking, as it inevitably does, Hal Cummings told of his efforts to ride an outlaw they had brought in from the Powder River country.

"I had a heap of trouble," said Hal, "gettin' my wood on him, and when I did get my tree laced up it didn't do me much good 'cause I didn't get settled before I goes sailin' off, flyin' low and usin' my face for a rough-lock till I lost 'nough hide to make a pair of leggin's."

Slug Cassell told of trying to ride a bronc that "warped his backbone and hallelujahed all over the lot." When asked what success he had he answered simply, "I went up to fork a cloud."

Laredo Cook once told of a rider who "got throwed so high when he came down he had St. Peter's initials whittled on his boot soles," and Zack Price admitted of a time when "I got throwed so high I could've said my prayers before I lit." Another told of a buster who "got throwed so high the birds built nests in his hair before he came down," and another made a similar statement when he said, "I was throwed so high I thought shore we'd find a nest of bluebirds in the seat of my pants when I came down." Once when Smoky Saddler was thrown pretty high, he tried to alibi by saying he "only wanted to go up and see what the moon was made of." At another time I heard a similar expression in West Texas — "I went up so high the bluebirds built nests in my pocket before I came down."

Other comments about horses that could buck high I have heard at various times and places include: "That hoss acted like he was tryin' to chin the moon"; "that bronc stuck his bill in the ground and tried to kick the teeth out of the man in the moon"; and "that hoss scraped a bird's wing as he went by." Buck Mitchell told of a ride he had by saying, "I was tryin' to smooth the humps out of that gut-twister, but he soon had me soarin' so high it was damned scary to a man without wings"; and Sam Dunlap, in telling of a ride he remembered, said, "I had to keep dodgin' my head to keep from bumpin' the stars and I was clawin' all the leather in sight." Another, in speaking of a horse bucking high, said, "That bronc blowed the plug out and made a balloon ascension." Still another said, "This hoss I'm ridin' swallowed his head and proceeded up to where the lights of Jerusalem shone. There we parted company and the bronc came down alone."

Often the bronc buster of a ranch would "top off"

a half-broken horse for another rider "to see that there ain't no bed-springs loose." At the beginning of such a ride Pike Keeler said, "That hoss seemed to find something on his nose he wanted to wipe off and when I reached for the saddle horn my arm was too short." "Chokin' the horn," "grabbin' the nubbin'," "pullin' leather," "squeezin' Lizzie," were terms for this act of holding the saddle horn. It is rather disgraceful for a professional rider to grab the saddle horn when riding. When one cowboy accused another of "chokin' the horn till it was blue in the face," this cowhand answered, "I'd rather pull the horn out by the roots than lose my saddle and go back to camp by hand." And some are like Frank Young who said, "I bought that saddle horn and paid for it, and if I want to pull it off it's nobody's business but mine." Another admitted he "kept his hand on the saddle horn so it'd be there when I needed it." One rider was said to be "hangin' onto the horn like a cub bear onto a roastin' ear." In "ridin' the shows" one would be disqualified for "chokin' the horn," but on the range there were no rules, only the opinion of one's fellow riders.

A bad horse will sometimes swell his middle up to keep the cinch from being tightened, and one cowhand said of such a horse he was trying to saddle that "it looked like I'd forgot to remove the watermelon before saddlin' up." Some bad horses squeal a lot when ridden, and after riding such a horse, Buck Hayes said, "With all that squealin' that hoss sounded like a hillbilly band out of tune." I have heard such expressions as, "that hoss hid his head and kicked the lid off," when speaking of a good bucker, or "it took a man with whiskers to ride 'im." Other expressions describing a good bucker were such as: "That bronc was pitchin' to beat a straight flush"; "it was like ridin' a cyclone with the bridle off"; "that hoss carnivaled all over the lot"; "that hoss jolted the savvy plumb out of him"; and "that hoss turned a wildcat." In speaking of such a bucker, Bill Reeves said, "For a minute I thought I'd mounted 'im backward for I shore as hell couldn't find his head."

Of a good rider it has been said that "he could shore curry the kinks out of a bronc's backbone." A man making a good ride never failed to bring out such compliments as: "He's stickin' like a tick makin' a gotch ear"; "he's stickin' like a fresh-water leech"; or "he screwed down in the saddle and stuck like a postage stamp." Slug Cassell once told of a good ride by saying, "That hoss hid his head and kicked the lid off, but it was just like buckin' off a porous plaster." When Dud Russell told of another ride, his admiration for the rider was expressed with, "You couldn't have chopped him loose from that hoss with an ax."

I have often heard references to poor riders with such comments as: "He musta learned to ride on a hobby hoss"; "he couldn't ride a covered wagon"; "he couldn't ride a pack hoss"; " he couldn't ride a cotton mule"; or "he couldn't ride nothin' wilder'n a wheel chair." In speaking of a poor bucker, one cowboy said, "He couldn't throw off a wet blanket."

In speaking of a ride he had attempted, Art Wood commented, "After that ride all I needed to make me a cripple was a handful of lead pencils." One buster speaking of trying to ride a "windmiller" (said of a horse swapping ends rapidly), said, "That hoss gave a better merry-go-round ride than you pay a nickel for at a carnival."

The cowboy had various ways of expressing himself in describing a rider being thrown, such as: "That hoss soon had him pickin' daisies"; or, if thrown head first it was, "That hoss throwed him forked-end up." Other such expressions were: "That hoss grassed him in a hurry"; "it wasn't long till that hoss started slattin' his sails and had him dirtyin' his shirt"; and, as one cowboy said, "I didn't get settled in the saddle before that hoss shore sent me on a fart knocker." Another said, "I felt like I'd been ridin' the roughstring with a borrowed saddle. I ached in a lot of new places." Earl Devers told of a rider being thrown with, " He left that hoss in a short, unscheduled flight." Another said, "That hoss had me tryin' to knock a hole in my vest with my chin." In telling of a rider being thrown pretty hard, another cowhand said the rider "made such a hole when he landed we thought he was borin' for water." George Fenton, in telling of a ride he had attempted, said that "the cantle of the saddle hit my caboose and I started for Mars." Another said, "That hoss throwed me farther than a Death Valley buzzard could smell a dry canteen." When describing a bucker that was rapidly swapping ends, a puncher said, "It wasn't long till I got up with two handsful of somethin' I didn't want." One cowboy told of his bunkie riding a bad horse with, "After he landed on that cactus patch it took a week to pluck 'im so he wouldn't look like a porcupine." Another described an unsuccessful ride with "three times he tackled that hoss and three times he took up a homestead." When a cowboy said, "That hoss was doin' his best to take me to church," a tenderfoot would not know what he was talking about, but the cowhand knew he was describing a violently bucking horse that was doing his best "to make a Christian out of you." When one was thrown it was said that "he got a chance to eat gravel without stoopin'."

One evening just at dusk on a ranch near Amarillo, Texas, a roan outlaw was driven up and hazed into the corral. Bud Appleton had promised to break him. The next morning Bud's bunkie sat watching him shave.

"Bud," he said solemnly, "you're wastin' a lot of good time dewlappin' yourself with that dull razor. That roan

out in the corral will buck them whiskers off. He'll take
that curl out of your hair too."

One day in the spring some of the boys went out to
drive in the saddle band, and when they got them back
to the home corral there was an unbranded grulla in the
bunch. He had no saddle marks on him so the "old man"
called for a volunteer to ride him.

Gotch Kelly eyed the horse a moment or two, then
climbed down off the fence.

"Ridin' that hoss'll be as easy as shootin' fish in a dry
lake. Put a rope on 'im boys while I get my leather."

"Says you," snorted Blackie Deason. "Give that hoss
a chance and he'll stomp you in the ground so deep you'll
take root and sprout."

Gotch made a good start. He did get both feet in the
stirrups, but when he smacked that horse on the "git up
end" it was not many jumps until he hit the ground and
lay still. When they picked him up he was, as one said,
"flat as a wet leaf and headed for a week in the bed wagon."

When a rider is thrown he rarely offers an alibi. If
he does it is one he expects no one to believe, such as Tank
Dennis offered when he said, "I started to fan that bronc,
but lost my hat and got off to look for it."

Sunfishing is a bucking term used to describe the
movements of a horse when he twists his body into a
crescent, alternately to the right and to the left; or, in
other words, when he seems to try and touch the ground
first with one shoulder and then the other, letting the
sunlight hit his belly. While watching one such horse
going through his antics, George Rogers remarked that
this horse was "showin' his belly like he was proud of it."

When another watched a horse pitching "fence-cor-
nered" (a style of bucking in which the horse zigzags much
as a frontier rail fence), he said, "That hoss is shore layin'
a rail fence." One rider, telling of riding a runaway bucker

remarked, "All I could do was just let 'im run down his mainspring." In speaking of fast horses I have heard such expressions as "he's as fast a hoss as ever looked through a bridle," and "he's ridin' a hoss that could outrun hell with its tail afire." When a rider had saddle sores, or perhaps a boil on his posterior, and was riding on the stirrups, he claimed he was "ridin' standin' up to save saddle leather."

The Texas cowboy rode a double-rigged saddle and had nothing but contempt for the center-fire saddle used by Californians because they were difficult to keep in place and therefore the horse's back was rubbed sore. Tex Fuller described such a ride with, "He's ridin' one of those lean-and-hungry saddles that's chewin' the hoss's back up."

When one was riding recklessly, he might be described as "ridin' like a deputy sheriff." When a cowman said someone was "ridin' for a blind bridle" he meant that this party was working for a homesteader, who, like most of them, used bridles with blinders, which were held in great contempt by the cowman. The expression was considered an insult.

Many a cowhand has been thrown when he was trying "to kick the frost out of some jughead," and no matter how he had "sunned his moccasins" you would be safe in betting that he would yell that familiar cry — "Ketch my saddle!"

# On The Prod

As a rule the early-day cowman kept a "dally" on his temper. He knew that hot words led to cold slabs if there were guns involved. For man or animal to be mad, it was said he was "ringey," "riled," "on the prod," "on the peck," "had his bristles up," "gets his back up," or "paints himself for war."

In the early days every man packed a gun, but he was not so quick to use it as some story writers would have us believe. You would find the cowhand very quiet with his words in a crisis. He was no coward, but he was not so bloodthirsty he would take a life for the defense of a little pride. He would shoot quick enough for self-protection, but would take a lot of ribbing before starting a "powder-burnin' contest." He had no hankering to "ride the highlines." When he did go after his gun he did so with a serious purpose. Every sense was keyed to shooting as fast and accurately as possible to make the first shot the last of the fight.

There are times in life when a man has to fight or lose his self-respect, and when two enemies met they immediately went into the gunman's crouch, leaning slightly forward with knees a little bent, hands near the gun butt, fingers spread and bent like bird claws, alert, every muscle tense — that familiar gesture, catlike and perilous. While each waited for the other to make the first move, native caution made the bystanders scud out of the way of future activities.

Sitting around a cow-camp listening to cowboy yarn spinning, one hears a lot of salty talk on all subjects, and fighting furnished many examples of the cowboy's aptness in his use of figures of speech. Around a campfire where outdoor men gather, it is a common occurrence to hear them tell of fights they have had, or of fights they have witnessed. When two men, toughened by hard outdoor life, and used to taking chances, get into a combat there is sure to be a "hide hung up." After one such fight Muley Metcalf described the loser as "He looked like he'd crawled through a bob-wire fence to fight a bob-cat in a briar patch"; and Ralph Crane said of another that "he was so skinned up his own folks didn't know him from a fresh hide." I think it was Jud Cramer who once told of a fight he had, in which he "lost 'nough hide to half-sole an elephant." Another said "he lost 'nough hide to make a saddle cover." Some cowhand might tell of a fighter getting "knocked cold 'nough to skate on," while a different yarn spinner might speak of another "losin' 'nough blood to paint a house."

I have heard many expressions depicting anger such as: "He's so mad he could bite himself"; "he's madder'n

a rained-on rooster"; "he's madder'n a drunk squaw";
"he's mad as a barkeep with a lead quarter"; "he's mad
'nough to kick his own dog"; "he's so mad he could bite
a gap out of an ax"; "he's mad 'nough to eat the devil
with his horns on"; "he's so mad he could swallow a
horned toad backward"; and "he's mad 'nough to kick
a hog barefooted."

Other expressions of anger I have heard at various
ranches by different groups of cowhands include: "He's
loaded to the muzzle with rage"; "he's sore as a scalded
pup"; "he's sullen as a soreheaded dog"; "he's sore as a
frog in a hot skillet"; "he's salty as Lot's wife"; "he's
salty as Utah"; "he's proddy as a locoed steer"; "he's cross
as a snappin' turtle"; "he's cross as a bear with two cubs
and a sore tail"; and "he's mad as a peeled rattler." But
when he got in a good humor again he was said to "get
over his frothy spell."

In speaking of a cowhand getting into a fighting
mood, I have heard such expressions as, "he paints himself for war"; "he digs up the tomahawk"; "he arches his
back like a mule in a hail storm"; "he starts sharpenin'
his horns"; "he digs up the tomahawk and goes on the
war-path"; "he's in a sod-pawin', horn-tossin' mood"; "he
paws up a little sand"; "he shuts his face hard 'nough to
bust his nutcrackers"; "he's grittin' his teeth like he could
eat the sights off a six-gun"; "he swelled up like a poisoned
pup"; and "he's hell bent for trouble." Tom Haines
described a friend getting into a fighting mood with, "He
lowered his horns at him and pawed up a little sand"; and
another described such a case with, "He pulled his hat
to a fighting' angle."

Jay Lacey told of a puncher who, he said, was "filin'
his teeth" for another puncher. "He don't say nothin',"
said Joe, "but it ain't safe to ask questions." Another
cowhand spoke of one who always seemed to be looking

for a fight with, "He'd crawl your hump at the drop of a hat and drop it himself." Anyone with a touchy disposition might be said to "act like he was raised on sour milk."

In telling of a fight he had had Jerry Harper said, "He used a language against me that I wouldn't take from nobody but my wife, so I combed his hair with the barrel of my six-gun." Another said, "I busted his talk-box and he had to go to the dentist to get his bridle teeth fixed." One cowboy said of a fight he had had, "I popped him between the horns and knocked his jaw back so far he could scratch the back of his neck with his front teeth." Another said, "I gave him a punch that shore knocked the core out of his Adam's apple," and still another gave a similar description, "I busted his Adam's apple, and he tasted apple juice till he got his cider mill workin' again."

A puncher of the Swinging L told another, whom he did not like, that "I'd like to look at you through the sights of a Winchester some day when the grave grass was growin' green." At another time I heard a puncher on the LX speak of an enemy with, "I promised myself that if I ever got him out on my range I'd squirt 'nough lead into him to make it a payin' job to melt him down." In telling of a time when the foreman of a ranch ran across a yearling with a blotted brand, Sam Bond commented that "when the boss saw that burned-over brand he was all horns and rattles."

Most fights were preceded by preliminary threats, and of these I have heard such examples as, "I'll knock you so far it'll take a week for a blood hound to find you"; "haul in your neck or I'll tromp your britches"; "wash off your war-paint or I'll fog you till you look like an angel in the clouds"; "pull in your horns, you don't scare nobody with bones in his spinal column"; "I'll kick your pants up 'round your neck so tight they'll choke you to death"; "I'll knock your ears down to where they'll do for wings"; "I'll collect 'nough of your hide to make a saddle cover"; "I'll put a head on you so big you can eat hay with the hosses"; "I'll kick you so hard you can buckle your belt 'round your neck"; and "I'll wipe you out like a nigger eatin' a saucer of lick." I heard one puncher say, "I'll clip your horns, you got too much spread," and the other answered, "Hop to it! There ain't nobody settin' on your shirt tail."

Sug Morgan told of a bully who tried to buffalo a puncher from the Turkey Track, but, he said, "This Turkey Track hand let him feel his gun barrel where his hair was thinnest, and put a knot on his head that'd sweat a rat to run around." Buck Weaver, in telling of a fight of an old-timer "who'd stood up to fight before he was weaned till he was as bowlegged as a barrel hoop," said, "He'd fight a rattler and give 'im first bite, and his scars was a regular war map," and, continued Buck, "this other party had some sensitive disposition himself and was impulsive with a gun. That fight made an ordinary fight look like a prayer meetin'. This first old-timer was hit, too, and when that fight was over he's as worn and weary as a fresh-branded calf, but he's still got strength 'nough to carve another scallop on his gun." Another, in describing a fight he had seen, said, "He gives this other pelican such a shake his bones rattled in his skin like throwin' down an armful of wood, and he's so skinned up he looked like the U.S. flag."

In the early days the cowboy used his gun when he got into a fight. He called fist fights "dog fights." After being in such a fight Carl Cook said, "No more of them dog fights for me. It ain't natural for a man to fight that way. If the Lord had intended men to fight like dogs He'd a-give us longer claws and sharper teeth."

I have heard cowboys, in telling of someone using the barrel of his six-gun as a club, use such descriptions as, "After gettin' his hair parted with that six-gun, he slept as gentle as a dead calf"; "he plowed a fire-guard through his scalp with a six-gun"; "he hit him so hard he couldn't answer St. Peter's questions"; and "after that lick he went down like a peck of wet fish nets." Other descriptions of one being "laid out" include: "He's laid out cold as a meat-hook"; "he folded him up like an empty purse"; "he knocked 'im cold 'nough to skate on"; "he walked up and down his backbone like he's climbin' a ladder"; and "he had 'im settin' on a damp cloud learnin' to play a harp."

To "hang up his hide," "clean his plow," or "sharpen his hoe" was to whip one. Hunting for trouble was "pawin' 'round for turmoil," and when that trouble developed it was said that "there was hell to pay and no pitch hot." Nate Baker, describing a fight on the V Up and V Down Ranch when passing the bunkhouse, declared, "It sounded like they was shoein' a bronc inside." In disarming an adversary another cowhand said, "I stripped him of the bric-a-brac he packed at his waist," and another described a gunfight with three against one by saying of the one that "he went through that gang like a cottontail rabbit through a briar corral."

Mickey O'Dowd was shot in the shoulder during a gun fight on the Box 7. The camp cook — like all range cooks — not only had to serve as banker, seamstress, father-confessor and dozens of other duties, but as a doctor as well. Mickey later spoke with pride of the cook's surgical aid and finished by saying, "Cookie was right there with the parin' knife when it comes to minin' for lead."

# Gunmen and Rustlers

SOME FOLKS THINK because a man wears a pair of boots and a big hat he is bound to be a cowboy. This kind of thinking is one reason the cowboy has been given a bad name. In the early days there were many men running the range who were not cowboys. The West was also a grazing ground for gunmen and desperadoes. These fellows hived up in town, not on the range. The range was too lonesome for their breed.

One old cowman spoke of the reign of outlaws in his section with, "Thieves and killers were so thick you'd think they had a bill-of-sale to the whole damned country." Another expressed the opinion that "the good citizens didn't like this breed and most of 'em died young." On this subject another old-timer remarked, "A mighty few of 'em got a chance to quit this life in bed with a preacher hoverin' over 'em and a doctor takin' their pulse count," and another said that "most of 'em were put to bed with a pick and shovel, and there wasn't nobody there to let 'em down easy with their hats off." As another expressed it, "There wasn't many tears shed at a Boot Hill buryin'," and one said, "Boot Hill's full of fellers that pulled their triggers before aiming."

In speaking of a gunman, I have heard cowboys use such expressions as, "he lived a life that'd make some of them scary yellow-back novels look like a primer," or "his past was full of black spots." When it was said that a man "wore his guns low" it meant that he was always ready to use them, and as one said, "A man that wears his guns low don't do much talkin' with his mouth." Another, in speaking of a gunman, said, "He's one of them hombres that packs his gun loose."

Duke Noel, in telling of a gunman he knew, remarked, "That hogleg hangin' at his side wasn't no watch charm, neither did he pack all that hardware for bluff nor ballast." I have heard heavily armed men described with: "He's packin' so much artillery it makes his hoss swaybacked," or "he packed so much hardware it gave him kidney sores." Some old long-haired badman "wearin' a load of hay on his skull," as one cowboy said, "spent his time tryin' to show how wild and wicked the West grew her men," and he might claim "he was the worst man west of any place east," but in the old days he frequently "wiggled his trigger finger once too often." However, as Jack Burnett once said, "You'd never find his kind settin' on his gun hand."

Describing the gunman, cowboys have said that "his finger had the trigger itch"; "he's got a sensitive disposition and is impulsive with a gun"; and, "he likes a shade start in the draw and ain't too good to get you from a sneak if he thinks he can get away with it, but the West's code of fair play puts the hobbles on most of his coyote work." Tom Kirk spoke of one as being "a wolf and he ain't togged out in no sheep's wool either." Some of those old gunmen "packed iron so long he felt naked when he took it off," but there were men in the West who "never packed an ounce of iron."

After participating in a gun fight, Carey Nelms said, "After that powder-burnin' contest my gun was emptier'n a banker's heart." Spot Davis, an old-timer, tough in his own right, told of a gunman jumping him one day. Spot said he bristled right back at him and told him, "You might be a man-eater, but you'll find me a tough piece of gristle to chaw." One cowhand, telling of a would-be badman who loved to scare a tenderfoot, said that "he would wild up with fierce looks and snorts and orate plenty savage of his bold, bad deeds"; and another described a like character as "one of them long-hairs who does his damndest to fertilize the cow country's reputation for bein' wild and woolly." When Tom Mercer said, "In that tough town there's a man for breakfast ever' mornin'," he meant there was a man killed there every night.

It was said of a gunman that "he liked to dabble in gore." These men had to be able to draw a gun fast to stay alive, and of an unlucky one it was said that "when he reached he fumbled and it was a fatal weakness." Another such expression was, "When the showdown came he was caught short."

Otto Crane, telling of a gunman who had married and reformed, remarked that "he hadn't shot nobody for so long his trigger finger went to sleep." Another puncher told of a gunman who was gunning for him and admitted that he "shore hunted a hole to fort up in." An old stage driver, recounting the time he was held up by some road agents, said, "I reached in the sky so high when my hands came down I had wild goose feathers 'tween my fingers." Chick Coleman described a cowhand trying to shoot up the town by saying that "he was doin' a good job of pullin' the town up by the roots till the marshall took all the slack out of his rope."

When a cowhand was hired by a ranch to do some fighting in its feud with another ranch, it was said of him that "he was drawin' fightin' wages and huntin' somebody to smoke up." A gunman was often referred to as being "hell on wheels," and when it was said of one that "he was one of them fellers with the pronto bug," it meant he was spending much of his time practicing a fast draw. When a man practiced drawing and snapping his gun without ammunition, it was called "dry shootin'."

An old saying of the early range was that all a man needed to start a brand of his own was "a rope, a runnin' iron and the nerve to use it." The struggle for existence on a fierce frontier developed the nerve, ropes and running irons were cheap, and cow thieves developed until rustling became quite an industry. A rustler was said to "have a sticky rope"; "pack a long rope"; "throw a big loop"; was "handy with the runnin' iron"; or was "careless with his brandin' iron." Sometimes it was said of him that "his calves don't suck the right cows"; "his cows have twins"; "his cows have a calf every wash day"; "he keeps his brandin' iron smooth"; "he ran a butchershop and got his cattle mixed"; or, if he killed the mother to steal the calf, he was said to "pin crepe on the kid."

Stealing unbranded cattle was the easiest, least dangerous, and therefore the most popular kind of rustling. Brand changing was easily botched, and often left telltale results that might cause the thief to be "invited to be the guest of honor at a string party." It took a great deal of skill to change a brand successfully, and the average cowhand was not expert enough to fool a real cowman very long.

Because the cattlemen themselves knew every trick of the cow thief, the rustler had to be smart enough to outwit them. He knew that his very neck depended upon his cunning. His constant danger sharpened his wits, and because he was the aggressor he did a lot of thinking about the cattlemen, much more than the cattlemen did about him. He was an adventurous soul to start with, and the excitement of the game was what he liked. He was usually honest in most other ways, and in the early days tried to take calves from those who would not be hurt too much by the loss.

A rustler usually started out in a small way. He was often some fellow who had become tired of working for thirty dollars a month while seeing his boss grow rich. Perhaps he first squatted on a little land and bought a few head of cattle as an excuse for being there. In riding over the range he saw no harm in putting his brand on a "slick" or two because he knew other men who had gotten their start that way and were now looked upon as solid citizens. Having gotten away with the first few thefts, his appetite was whetted for owning a herd large enough to make him independent. This is where he made his big mistake, for it was a rare case when one was satisfied with the gradual building up of a herd. And once he was placed under suspicion he was watched, and sooner or later the smartest of them slipped up.

In the early days of the unfenced range, when the big ranches were run by Eastern and foreign capital and absentee owners, and the country was full of mavericks, it was easy to steal oneself into the cattle business. With the crowding of the range and the organization of stock associations with their stock inspectors, it became harder and harder. But there is always someone who thinks he can get away with it, and cattle are still being stolen, just as banks are still being robbed in spite of the fact that the James boys have been dead for many years.

Bud Taylor said of one rustler, "Maybe he couldn't see whose calves he was ketchin', but he could shore see where to slap his brand." Another rustler was described as one who "would steal the ball from a crippled tumble-bug and start him on the wrong road home"; and still another as, "He'd steal acorns from a blind sow and then kick her for squealin'." It was said of one reformed rustler that "he quit rustlin' for the good of his gullet." When a cowman spoke of a rustler by saying: "He spent a few years playin' checkers with his nose," he meant that this individual spent those years in prison.

When Skeeter Brooks told of finding some hides buried in the river he said, "When we found those hides ever'one of 'em's got a stovepipe hole, and we knew somebody's runnin' a meat wagon of our beef." By stove-pipe hole he meant that the brand had been cut out of the hide to hinder identification.

In telling of a bunch of rustlers that had been caught, Chick Coleman commented, "They lost their voices explainin' to so many different judges how they'd come to have their brands on somebody else's cows."

The horse thief was the lowest of all thieves and his career was usually ended in a "strangulation jig." One cowboy said of such a man, "He couldn't resist pickin' up a rope that somehow had a hoss fastened to the other end of it when he got home"; and it was said of another that "he admired other folk's hoss flesh too much."

There were times in the early West when the rope was resorted to as a final justice; but no man living there made it more than an occasional subject of conversation, nor would he admit that he had anything to do with one. These were mighty stern and solemn affairs and not subject to jests or popular mention.

A hanging was spoken of as a "necktie social," "strangulation jig," or "lynchin' bee"; and the victim was said to have "died of throat trouble"; "he had a case of hemp fever"; "they had him gurglin' on a rope"; "had him playin' cat's cradle with his neck"; or "had him lookin' through cottonwood leaves."

Though lynchings were not common, when a posse did catch an outlaw or horse thief, "They made a cottonwood blossom out of him," as one cowhand said. In telling of a known rustler, Jack Kelly commented, "He was doin' his best to ride under a cottonwood limb and do a strangulation jig." Speaking of the hanging of a certain rustler, one cowboy said, "When they caught him blottin' a brand they left him doin' a mid-air dance from a cottonwood." Describing the lynching of a horsethief, another cowhand said that "his neck was too damned short and they took him out to stretch it." In a similar vein John Dorsey told of one with, "They tied him to a tree but forgot and tied him so high his feet wouldn't reach the ground."

I have also heard such expressions as: "They hung him up to dry"; "they used him to trim a tree"; "they had him lookin' up a limb"; "they hung him so high he could look down on the moon"; and in telling of a hanging one cowboy said, "It was a case of a stiff rope and a short drop." I have also heard such expressions as "they gave him a chance to look at the sky." One cowboy, telling of a friend trying to get him to help rustle some cattle, added, "I told him I didn't have no hankerin' to ride under a cottonwood limb." Another said he was "too proud of my Adam's apple to want to be exalted." The expression to "telegraph him home" was to use the rustler's own rope and borrow a pole from Western Union. More than one man who has admired other people's stock has "climbed the Golden Stairs on a rope." When a cowman referred to someone with, "He died in a horse's nightcap," he meant that the one spoken of was hanged. The same thing might be expressed by another with, "They soon had him doin' a Texas cakewalk."

# Riding the Highlines

WHEN A COWHAND FALLS from grace and "stampedes to the wild bunch" it is not long until he is "just two jumps ahead of a sheriff." And once he starts "ridin' the highlines," as Chuck Neeley said, "he is forced to ride over trails that'd make a mountain goat nervous, and in a country so rough an ordinary man couldn't find his saddle seat with a forked stick."

Many a "long rider" got tired of "usin' his back for a mattress and his belly for a coverin'" before he could find an open trail out of the country. And if he did not know you as a friend, as Lonny Norris remarked, "you couldn't get close 'nough to him to borrow a chaw." Dewlap Burdick said of such a man that "he's one of those fellers that keeps his hoss wonderin' at the hurry they're in, and he don't leave 'nough tracks to trip an ant." Russ Harrison said of another, "When he hits the breeze for a healthier climate he don't stop for no kissin'." Another spoke of one with, "Where his hoss is goin' he don't know, but it's a cinch they won't be late"; and Spike Dodson, in telling a similar story, said, "He's makin' so much dust it don't settle all day."

When Rusty Combs said of a man that "he got a hankerin' to sniff gulf breeze and rolled his tail south," his listeners knew that the one spoken of was a "wanted" man making for the Mexican border. Slick Watson described such a man as "packin' a pair of them bring-'em-close glasses, and when he sees a posse on his trail he starts fixin' for high ridin'."

In telling of a sheriff and an outlaw having an exchange of shots before the latter started leaving the country, Spike Casey said, "Him and the sheriff swapped lead then had a hoss race." Ted Jenkins said such a man "was a thorn in the sheriff's shortribs, and kept him ridin' the hocks off his hoss." Bill McQueen remarked that when such a man "starts pullin' his freight for the tules he don't pay no more attention to distance and fatigue than a steer does to cobwebs." Most men do not like history too near home, but a man of this breed is usually kept "on the end of a runnin' iron until he couldn't settle long 'nough to call any place home." Jake Lane said of such a man, "With some posse campin' on his trail till he got saddle sores, he didn't get much chance to grow up with the country."

Tuck Roan told of one suspected of rustling by saying, "The cowmen took down their ropes and he headed in the direction advised by Mister Greeley"; and Rod Weber said of another old lawless Texan, "Because he happened to be an earlier riser than the sheriff and rode a faster hoss, he wasn't hung before he left Texas." Another told of a cowhand who "came whippin' a mighty tired hoss out of Texas," but when he was quizzed on the ranch he answered, "I didn't have to leave Texas. The sheriff came to the state line and just *begged* me to come back."

Many lawless men and gunmen came West in the early days because, as Sundown Shelby observed, "There was a longer distance between sheriffs." Another cowhand spoke of such a character with, "He left home in such a hurry he forgot to take his right name along"; and another said, "Their name seldom tallied with the family Bible." Of such men one cowhand commented that "these fellers change their names as easy as an Injun breaks camp."

Harold King said he became suspicious of a fellow rider when they were riding the range because "he kept his eyes on the horizon like he was expectin' a sheriff to bulge up on him." Dale Pitts said of another gunman that "he pulled for the Rio Grande because he had a hankerin' to go south in the yucca country where the lizards are out all winter." When a westerner spoke of another with such phrases as "he spent his time among the willows," or "he was spendin' his time ridin' the coulees," or "he was doin' his waterin' at night," he meant that this person was dodging the law. It was said of such a person "he wasn't on speakin' terms with the law."

One former outlaw commented that a certain town "didn't look like no health resort as long as that sheriff spread his blankets there"; and another admitted that when passing through a certain town "he kept his hat well down over his eyes as he's not sure if they still have the same sheriff they had a few years back." Once when one of the hands of the L7 came riding back to the ranch from town all excited and his horse in a lather, he was asked what the trouble was, and he answered he had "just had a run-in with one of them high grass constables."

When one of the Two-Pole Pumpkin cowhands got into a little trouble in town he was afraid to go back to the ranch for fear the law would seek him there. He admitted that he "covered his back with his belly and did a little sage-hennin'" that night, meaning that he was forced to stay overnight on the prairie without blankets. Another admitted that in his earlier wild days he "had to belly through the brush till he was as worn and weary as a fresh-branded calf." When such a character, as one cowboy said, "was ridin' a hoss and bein' followed by a sheriff-lookin' man, this seemed to have a stimulatin' effect on his rate of travel." If such a follower really was the sheriff, this outlaw, as Frank Hill said, "stirred up more dust in five minutes than Noah's flood could settle in forty years."

# Bucking Out in Smoke

THE COWBOY'S LIFE was daily full of peril, and he had
many close calls with death from various causes. Some
might come from gunplay, some from falling horses or
mad cows, some from stampedes, flooded rivers, quick-
sands or a thousand other causes. Lafe Wheeler, telling
of a man who seemed to attract danger, said, "For a man
who's gone through so many close shaves, I don't see how
he ever saved his whiskers." Chuck Neeley, relating a close
call he had in a gun fight, swore that his enemy's bullet
"came so close it raised a blister." Lonny Norris, speaking
of a time he was knocked out by a horse falling on him,
discovered he was still in the land of the living when he
"woke up and didn't hear harps nor smell smoke," and

Dunk Goss, in the dangerous path of a stampede, said he "heaved a prayer in the general direction of Heaven and *rode.*"

After coming out of some perilous situation, the cowboy has been heard to say he had been "near 'nough to hell to smell smoke." In the early days tragic death was of common occurrence, and perhaps to the outsider the cowboy did not seem to have the proper reverence for the mysterious future. He referred to death as the "misty beyond"; "death's got the runnin' iron on him brandin' him for the eternal range"; "he's sacked his saddle"; or said that "the grass is wavin' over him." To him death meant to "buck out," "cash in," "take the big jump," "pass in his chips," "go over the range," "lay 'em down," "shake hands with St. Peter," "take his place with the angels," or "he got a halo gratis."

The story of a killing was always a fascinating subject around a cow camp. If the listener did not know the deceased he knew someone who did. I have heard a good many unique expressions with reference to a killing that perhaps sound sacreligious to an outsider, but the cowboy did not mean them to be so. No occasion seemed to put the bridle on his native humor and exaggerations. Among the old-timers there were a good many who always seemed to be in trouble. It was said of them that they were "raised with a gun in one hand and a milk bottle in the other"; and Tex Biggers once spoke of such a man as one who "cut his teeth on a cartridge and stood up to fight before he was weaned till he was bowlegged as a barrel hoop." When one of those old fellows "digs for his blue lightnin' and unravels some cartridges," or "sets his gun a-goin' and burns some powder," somebody at the other end usually gets "fogged till he looks like an angel in the clouds." During range wars more than one horse has been sent home with its rider "strapped on, toes down."

When one met death in a prairie fire, it was "fried gent," "no breakfast forever," or "the long trail to Kingdom Come." When one died or was killed on the trail he was said to "land in a shallow grave" because usually the ground was rocky and the time was too short to dig a deeper grave.

Death itself came in for many unusual descriptions such as: "He's deader'n a can of corned beef"; "he's deader'n hell in a preacher's back yard"; "he wins a pitchfork for the eternal beyond"; "he's deader'n a six-card poker hand"; or "he's dead as Santa Ana and branded for the eternal range." One cowboy described a corpse he had found on the prairie with, "He lays there starin' at the sky, but seein' nothin'."

In the early days guns were a necessary part of the cowboy's accouterment, but the carrying of weapons gave many people the wrong impression of him. Those guns were not carried solely for the purpose of killing men. There were many other needs for them, such as wolves and snakes to be killed, and crippled stock or mad dogs to be shot, when having a gun meant the difference between life and death. There were times, too, when a gun was needed for giving signals. But, naturally, men carrying weapons found them useful in settling their quarrels.

I have heard various cowhands tell of some acquaintance being killed in a gun battle with such expressions as: "He got a case of lead poison"; and if shot in the head it was: "He put a window in his skull," or "he blowed his lamp out." If one was slow in drawing his gun and got killed, it was "another case of slow and he took his place with the angels." Another might say: "He fell all spraddled out, too dead to skin." One cowhand described a killing in a saloon by saying, "He passed in his chips with sawdust in his beard."

Through the years I have jotted down many descriptions of someone who had been considerably shot up, such as: "They had to pick him up with a blotter"; "his hide was so full of holes it wouldn't hold hay"; "he was so full of lead they took him to a smelter instead of the undertaker"; "he was so full of holes he wouldn't float in brine"; and "he was as full of holes as a cabbage leaf after a hail storm." One cowhand on the Fiddleback Ranch expressed the same thought with, "He's so full of lead they had to take him to a sinker factory." Another said, "There wasn't 'nough of him left to make a bull fighter's flag." "There wasn't 'nough of him to cram into an empty shell," said another. "They wiped him out like a nigger eatin' a saucer of lick," and "they didn't leave 'nough of him to snore," are other expressions I have heard.

Similar expressions in describing death by gunfire include: "They sent him to Heaven to take harp lessons"; "they had him fingerin' music out of a harp"; "they let sunshine through him like a pane of glass"; "they had him takin' off his spurs at the Pearly Gates"; "they had him settin' on a damp cloud learnin' to play a harp"; "had him goin' through the narrow part of Death Canyon"; or "sent him hoppin' over hot coals in hell."

Llano Pierce, describing the execution of a prisoner in Old Mexico, said that "they 'dobe walled him into Kingdom Come"; another, describing a critically wounded man who requested that his boots be removed before his passing, said, "He wanted to take the big jump without bein' weighted down with his boots"; and Charlie Bracken spoke of the death of an old cowman with, "He was eighty-two when he finished his circle."

Perhaps it was said of the deceased that "he went to hell on a shutter." If one shot another in the stomach, "he gave him a pill in the stomach he couldn't digest"; if he was considerably shot up "he was as full of lead as Joplin and Galena." A "corpse and cartridge occasion" of magnitude, where "the air was as full of lead as a bag of bullets," and where several men were killed, was described as looking "like beef day at an Indian agency." If any of the participants were wounded and still lived, they were "sent to the saw-bones to have the lead mined out." Jim Logan's way of telling you of a man getting shot was that "he leaned against a bullet goin' past."

One cowhand told of an acquaintance firing his gun at an enemy until it was empty with, "He fired till there wasn't a bean left in the wheel." Other expressions on this subject I have gathered are such as: "After that feud the undertaker was ridin' high on the wave of prosperity"; and of one who had been considerably shot up but still kept his feet, Hank Buckner said that "he packed lead like a grizzly bear"; and another spoke of one being shot several times with, "He was so filled with lead he couldn't walk uphill."

A deputy sheriff, telling of a time he was on his stomach behind a slight hill shooting it out with an outlaw he was trying to capture and had barely been missed, remarked, "When that bullet kicked dust in my face I wasn't slow in changin' my bedground." Another agreed that "whinin' lead is a hint in any man's language."

One might say of a man who had been shot that "a bullet nailed him down"; and I heard one cowboy say he shot another "where he looked biggest"; and another told of one talking himself into trouble with, "He augured himself into a cold-meat wagon." In shooting at another's feet one might say that "he built a smoke under his hoofs"; and Ed Foley told of a time he shot at some petty thieves by saying he "throwed a little gravel into their boots as they stampeded down the trail."

Tommy Pierce, describing an old-timer shooting a shotgun with an extra heavy recoil, said, "When he lets that load of buckshot go he had to stand spraddle-legged to keep from losin' his britches." Another spoke of the poor shooting of a friend with, "He couldn't hit anything with a shotgun loaded with packsaddles"; and a man hunting trouble is said to be "pawin' 'round for turmoil."

# Old Timers

In the cow country a man experienced in the cattle business may be called old even if he is young in years. But what most called an old-timer was both old in years and in experience. As he grew older and "put more wrinkles on his horns," he had "to take plenty hair off the dog" before he was classed with the old-timer who had become bone-seasoned by years in the saddle.

"He rode a runnin' iron for a stick hoss," was the way Phil Larson spoke of one who was raised to the cow business, and Dean Deming said of an experienced old cowman that "the cow business is an open book to him and he knows ever' leaf in 'er." I have heard another described as one who "might be old but he ain't hung up his saddle yet," meaning that the old fellow was still able to do some riding. Another expressed the same thought with, "He might be gettin' long in years, but his horns ain't never been sawed off."

In describing an old fighting cowman Don Weaver said, "He's cut his teeth on a cartridge and stood up to fight before he was weaned." Pokey Olsen, describing one old-timer who had been a fighter in his day, said, "His scars was a regular war map." An aged cowman might be "gettin' long in tooth," or "wrinkled as a burnt boot," but if he was a good one "he was a cowman from the boot heels up." I heard one old-timer start a yarn of reminiscences with the comment, "That takes me back to the days I was still bawlin' for skimmed milk."

After fences, most of these old-timers, as one said, "were always bellyachin' with a yearnin' to go somewhere where they could spread a loop without gettin' it caught on a fence-post." Concerning one such old fellow Jerky Raynor remarked that "he'd been in this country so long he knew all the lizards by their first names, except the younger set."

Down in Arizona I met an old desert rat, and after I had left him Cut-Bank Tuttle informed me, "That old wrinkle-horn's been gopherin' in these hills since Sittin' Bull was a calf." Some of the old fellows tottering around on bowlegs weakened from many years in the saddle have been described in many different ways, such as: "He's so bowlegged a yearlin' could run between his legs without bendin' a hair"; "he's bowlegged as a finger ring"; "he's so bowlegged he couldn't head a hog in an alley"; and Ed Frazier once described such a man by saying, "He's had a hoss under him so long his legs are warped." Another described Old Man Jensen as "bein' so bowlegged he couldn't change socks." Center-Fire Mahan pointed out an old man to me and said, "That old alkali's forked a hoss so long he straddles chairs instead of settin' like a human";

and Buck Weaver used to kid a good-natured old buck-nun in Texas and tell him he was "so bowlegged he couldn't set in an arm-chair."

The cowman has uttered some interesting phrases, too, in his references to the kids of the range. Ransom Fox referred to one as being "just a yearlin' that hadn't cut his tobacco teeth," and Ben Langford mentioned another that was "just fryin' size, but he'd inherited a lot of cow savvy from his old man." Dutch Roeder bragged that his own kid "had been ridin' for the ranch ever since he'd shed his milk teeth." Bill Hale, in speaking of his pampering a kid nephew, said, "I'll bet he hadn't been so humored since he wore three-cornered pants." Rocky Rhodes told of another that "had his folks buffaloed since before he quit wearin' folded pants"; and another puncher described a youngster who was beginning to feel his oats with, "He's shore got the growin' itch."

Every tenderfoot was fresh meat for the cowhand, and "stringin' a greener" was a favorite sport of the cow country. Some "stall-fed tenderfoot," if from the city, might be described as, "He's never been closer to a cow than a milk wagon," or similarly, "He's never been closer to a cow than a T-bone steak." I remember Guy Trimble describing one with, "He's a green pea if I ever saw one."

To the cowboy of today the Indian is more or less a dim tradition, but to the old-timer he was a red reality. The early-day cowhands, especially those who drove cattle over the trail, often came in contact with the Indians of their section. One old-timer used to tell of an occasion when he met a Comanche war party and did not let his conscience bother him when he "high-tailed it while the gate was still open," because "I didn't have no hankerin' to let them redskins undo my hairpins and cause my scalp to migrate to some koo-stick."

Another old-timer, in speaking of a half-breed, instead of merely stating that the subject was a half-breed, used the typically picturesque manner of description by saying, "his folks on his mother's side wore moccasins." Joe Nord once remarked that a certain half-breed was "Injun 'nough to get homesick in a skin lodge," and another described a half-breed as "Injun 'nough in his ways to have an eagle feather braided in his mane."

During a discussion of the government's policy of trying to civilize the Indian by making a farmer of him, Concho Bates snorted his opinion that "an Injun couldn't raise nothin' but hell and hair." Of course the Indian's scalping of his victim was the thing most dreaded by the white man, and much of the latter's references to the Indian referred to this act. Old man Nat Eklund, in telling of a scalping he had witnessed, said, "That Injun gave him a haircut with all the trimmin's," and another old-timer described a close call he had had with, "Them Injuns were tryin' to find out how I wore my hair." Another, telling of a close call with a group of warriors, said, "I had the fastest hoss and didn't give 'em a chance to take out my stopper and examine my works."

# Range Calico

THE EARLY WEST was a man's country. Until it became
more settled, "range calico was as scarce as sunflowers on
a Christmas tree," as one cowhand said. In later years
more married men came out to the range, bringing their
families. If there was a pretty daughter, as one cowhand
put it, "The whole range would soon be sufferin' with
Cupid's cramps," and some favored puncher "would be
callin' on her as regular as a goose goes barefooted." The
cowman called courting "gallin'," "ridin' herd on a
woman," "settin' the bag," "callin'," or "cuttin' a rusty";
or he was said to have the "calico fever." When the cowman
spoke of another "rotten loggin'," he meant he was out
"sparkin'" some woman on a log in the moonlight.

The shyness and awkwardness of a puncher in love might be expressed with, "She-stuff shore makes a peeler get his spurs tangled up," or, "That naked little runt with the bow and arrow can shore bugger up a cowboy." Toby Young told of a love-sick cowhand trying to court a waitress in town and said, "He used to ride to town ever' chance he got to spend his wages on pies and throat-ticklin' truck, eatin' like a hoss balin' bunchgrass till he developed a chronic case of bellyache, all because there's a biscuit-shooter workin' there that's easy on the eyes." At a different time another cowhand told of a friend who, "when he went a-courtin', her old man had to pour water on the front steps to keep him from settin' there all night." Dutch Akard told of another by saying that "after he meets this gal he swears there's a mistake in the census report and there ain't but one gal in the U.S."

No breed of men on earth respected a good woman more than the range man, and he did not censure the woman of the redlight district. As one cowhand observed, "In spite of their fancy clothes and fast ways, most of these gals had their hearts in the right place"; and another expressed a like sentiment with the comment that "she was livin' in the badlands where the lights are red and the carpets soft, but she was too good to be out with the strays." Another spoke of such a woman with, "She'd strayed off the main trail away from the home corral before her soul got its full growth"; and aonther woman was described as being "like the gal that'd got his bankroll the last time he was in town, and was waitin' with her paint and glad smile to trim him again." And speaking of a painted woman, one old cowboy described one such with, "She was one of those women that couldn't turn pale even when she's scared on account of a paint job that'd make an Injun jealous." Describing some dance hall girls in town, Gene Farrow said that "those gals didn't wear much more than a sneeze and a ring"; and of another it was said "she's been used to runnin' with the drags of the she-herd."

The grass widow is a dangerous "critter" for the bachelor cowboy. One described her as "a widow of the grass variety, but she don't let none of it grow under her feet"; and another told of one with, "That grass widow didn't have no trouble findin' a rake to gather her hay crop." The Heart and Hand woman was another who sometimes came West "to shake her rope at some lonely batch." She got this name from that old magazine put out by a matrimonial agency. Some love-hungry cowboy would get a copy through the mail and read it with a lot of interest, and his simple soul believed all its descriptions. He did not believe you could print anything that was not the truth. At one time the cowman depended upon those matrimonial bureaus for a wife like he did the mail-order houses for his winter underrigging. One cowhand said, "She's one of those catalog widows that wants her weeds plowed under." Sometimes she sent a picture, but as one recipient remarked, "The photograph she sent didn't show up all the blemishes."

A homely woman might "have a face built for a hackamore," or "she ain't nothin' for a drinkin' man to look at," but chances are "he wasn't no parlor ornament either." A stout woman would likely be described with such phrases as, "she's got so much tallow she's big 'nough to hunt bears with a switch," or "she was beef plumb to the hocks."

When a cowman married it was said that "he slapped his brand on her and tied her to the snortin' post"; "he mortgages his here and hereafter for the papers necessary to file a permanent claim on her affections, and the sky-pilot welds 'im to the neck-yoke"; or "he dropped his rope on her, threw her into the home pasture and nailed the gate shut"; and "he runs the smokin' brand of matri-

mony on her and she's been wearin' the bell ever since."
Such a man was said to be "hogtied with matrimonial
ropes."

At a ranch dance, perhaps some of the city girls
attended, and as one cowboy said, "Those city gals shore
boogered up the range heifers, because they were dressed
in style, with silks and satins that swished till they sounded
like high wind in tall grass." Perhaps this swish was because
"gals in those days didn't show much of their fetlocks."
Cash Jameson told of an old bachelor falling for a widow
with: "He was an old buck-nun who'd never been hogtied
with matrimonial ropes, and he didn't savvy she-stuff,
but after this widow plucks the emblem of bondage from
the third finger of the hand she'd once give away, she had
'im walkin' the fence." Another such character was
described with: "He got plumb dissatisfied with the old
boar's nest he'd been livin' in when this little filly cut his
trail." Of one widow it was said that "she might have a
short rope, but she threw a wide loop." Of another, one
cowboy said that "the only evidence of her husband's
passin' was the black weeds his widow cultivated for a
week or two."

One love-sick cowboy described a school teacher by
saying, "That little wisdom-bringer's so sweet bee trees
are gall beside her"; and I heard another say of his girl
friend that "her eyes are as soft and leathery as blackstrap
lick poured onto a tin plate." One cowboy, speaking of his
bunkie in love, said, "When he starts talkin' about her
bein' as pure as the Christmas snow we knew it wouldn't
be long till she'd be puttin' the hobbles on his freedom."
"When a filly starts draggin' her rope for a man," commented Buck Mason, "it won't be as long as a summer
day in Yuma till she's got him trottin' in double harness."
When a woman from the East came West and married a
cowman, some native son was apt to say that "she soon

had him so civilized he'd tote an umbrella and wear galluses," or that "she soon had him so bridle-wise he'd stand hitched with the reins hangin' down."

Of a crabbed old maid a cowboy on the T Anchor said, "She was soured on life and couldn't get the acid from her system"; and another described a talkative woman by remarking that "she was in the lead when tongues were given out." Other opinions of women as expressed by cowmen are such as: "I'd as soon watch a bag of fleas as a woman," "you can't turn a woman no more'n you can a runaway hog," or "you couldn't check her with a three-quarter rope and a snubbin' post."

Two old bachelor cowboys were discussing the women they knew who were eligible for marriage. Bill had the "calico fever" bad. In plain words he wanted to get married. There was a very fat woman over on Salt Creek, and Bill's friend suggested her as a possible prospect.

"She ain't so good lookin' and kinda looks like she was weaned on a pickle," said Jim, "but after all beauty's only skin deep."

"Hell," grunted Bill, "she's got too much skin. Four more pounds and she could join a sideshow."

In speaking of a widow with a half dozen kids, Bill Taylor said, "I'd just as soon marry an orphan asylum"; and of another, Ted Young remarked that "she had 'nough kids to start a public school." A jealous woman was described as "jealous as a hound with her first litter of pups." I heard another cowhand describe a woman as "soft and fluffy as a goose-hair pillow, but icicles are plumb feverish compared to her." One old bachelor who got tired of his own cooking, married and said, "Leave it to a female to put flavor in your grub." His friends, however, said of him that "he was at the age when he should've been forgettin' the she-stuff and spend more time reflectin' on his wasted youth."

I used to talk with a couple of cowhands on a ranch in West Texas, and they always brought a friend they called Curly into the conversation.

"Curly got his name," said one of them, "because he had about as much hair as a Mexican dog, and they're fixed for hair like a sausage. The whole top of his head was as clean as a baby's leg, and when he took off his hat it looked like a full moon on the rise. Curly savvied a cow till he knew what she said to her calf, but he was sufferin' from two incurable diseases. He had the calico fever and the saddle itch. Those two complaints could never pull with even tugs."

The second cowhand added, "If he could've gotten the tumbleweed blood out of his system he could've been a top hand as a rancher. He wanted some calico hangin' on his clothesline worse'n any man I ever saw, but he wouldn't settle down long 'nough to put up that clothesline."

"He was old 'nough to be our dad," continued the first speaker, "and I wonder to this day why he took us under his wing. From the very first he took to us like honeysuckle to a front porch."

"He had some kind of influence over us," the second speaker went on, "and whenever he wanted to pull his picket pin and drift we'd follow him like a remuda follows a bell mare."

## Some Typical Cowboy Expressions

To BE AN ALL AROUND good cowboy one had to have some
ability at tracking and at reading sign. A great deal of the
excellence of the early-day cowboy depended upon this
ability and he took great pride in such talent. Every track
told him a story plainer than if it had been printed in a
book. By his ability at reading sign a good cowhand could
save his ranch time, money, horseflesh, and sometimes his
own life as well. He could tell by the tracks if a horse
was shod or barefooted, if he was walking or running, if
he was being driven in a hurry, or was grazing or going
in a walk. He could tell by the twigs and bushes and
the bent grass approximately how long ago an animal had
made the track.

A cowboy riding down the trail might seem to be half asleep to an outsider, but his eyes missed nothing. If he saw cattle spread out and grazing, he knew everything was "hunky-dory," but a bawling cow showing nervousness was a sign her calf was dead or in trouble. If he came across an animal with thin flanks, a swollen jaw and drooping head, it was a sign she had stopped a rattlesnake's fangs. When he saw an animal with a nervous twitching hide he knew it was a sign of screw worms.

Reading sign generally refers to tracking, but all of the following come under this heading: A cowman can see a rider from a great distance and tell whether that rider is a white man or an Indian. The white man would be riding straight up and straight legged; the Indian would be swinging a quirt and digging his heels into the horse's belly at every step. When the wagon boss, on roundup, caught his best circle horse, the cowhand did not need words to tell him a big circle was going to be made. When the boss took the top horse from a cowboy's string, he knew that the boss was telling him stronger than words that he wanted him to quit before he got fired. On a clear day the cowman did not need a watch to tell the time of day: he could tell directions at night by the stars; he could tell a change in the weather by watching the action of the cattle; and he could even tell what state a man was from by the clothes he wore, especially by his hat and the way he wore it. Words were not needed to tell a range man a lot of things.

What he called "sign" were tracks and other evidence of their passing left by animals or men. The act of interpreting these markings in following a trail was called "reading sign." To "cut for sign" was to examine the ground for tracks or droppings, and when those signs were clearly visible it was a "plain trail." When the sign was old and indistinct it was a "blind trail," or "cold trail," and the vernacular for following a trail so clearly marked that it could not be lost was called "sliding the groove." The cowman often used his trail vernacular in ordinary conversation, and in speaking of someone deceiving another the former was described as "clouding the trail." When he was following someone he was said to be "camping on his trail." When his immediate duty was to ride the range to follow animals that had strayed too far and turn them back, or pull cattle from bogholes, turn them away from loco patches, or do anything else in the interest of his employers, he was said to be "riding sign."

I have heard many expressions concerning a man's tracking ability, or the lack of it. Spindle Stetts used to tell of a man that "could follow a wood tick on solid rock in the dark of the moon." Kirk Myers claimed of another that he "had a nose so keen he could track a bear in runnin' water"; and Pima Norton once said of his bunkie that "when it comes to readin' sign he could track bees in a blizzard." One cowboy said of another, "He could track a tapeworm lookin' for a home."

On the other hand, there are some men who, it seemed, could not develop close observation and tracking ability. Slim Siegal once said of such a man that "he couldn't find a calf with a bell on in a corral." Bud Boliver said of a similar type, "He couldn't find a baseball in a tomato can"; and at another time I heard one say that "he couldn't track a wagon through a boghole." There was a cowhand up in the Dakota Badlands whom Lonesome Wier claimed "couldn't follow a load of loose hay across a forty-acre field of fresh snow"; and Homer King expressed the same thought with, "He couldn't track an elephant in three feet of snow."

Speed, especially in horses, is a subject often discussed around campfires. Nearly every puncher has a horse in his string that he claims is "as fast a hoss as ever looked through a bridle." Cap Hunt once stated that a fast horse he admired was "leadin' that race like an antelope would a hog"; and on another occasion I heard Zen Miller describe a horse that was able to "throw dirt in the face of a jackrabbit." Another rider told of leaving the country when he "pushed on the reins till he had that hoss kickin' the jackrabbits out of the trail."

This speed in horses has been expressed with many original phrases. Some I have heard are: "He's goin' like hell in a hand basket"; "he fogs down the road like he's goin' to a dance"; "he was draggin' his navel in the sand from who laid the chunk"; "he don't lose no time flaggin' his kite"; and "he punched the breeze and traveled faster'n bad news at a church social."

If you have seen a cloud of dust raised by the horse of a rider traveling at high speed in the desert country it will not be hard for you to understand why the men of the Southwest, speaking of such a rider, would say "he shore is a-foggin' it," "he's burnin' the trail some," or "he's shore skippin' through the dew." Also in describing an animal's speed a cowhand might say that "he shore naveled the sand"; "if he humps himself much more he'll shore set his belly a-smokin'"; or "he's goin' like the heelflies are after him."

Cut-Bank Tuttle once told of riding a race in which his horse passed the others "so fast they looked like they were backin' up." In speaking of a man running on foot Bull Grimes stated that "he humped his tail at the shore end and made far apart tracks," while Blue Yeager spoke of another "runnin' like the devil with a tar bucket." Ranicky Reynolds, telling of a friend trying to escape the rush of a mad cow in a branding pen said, "He was shore heatin' his axles and doin' his best to keep step with a rabbit." In another section of the country Bill Keith, telling a similar story, had his friend "hobbled with a pair of hairy chaps, but he couldn't have made better time if he'd been stripped to the buff."

Bucky Wilcox described the sudden departure of a certain man with, "He quit us like a scorpion had crawled down his neck." Another such expression was: "They left like a trail herd goin' for water," or "he took off like a gut-shot wolf." One cowhand told of a bunch of cowboys in town in trouble with the town marshal. In describing the action when this officer began to shoot, he said that "them fellers scattered like a night stampede."

A fast runner, either man or horse, might be said to be "movin' faster'n a squirrel in a cage"; "burnin' the breeze from who laid the chunk"; "he's goin' like the clatter wheels of hell"; "he could outrun hell with its tail afire"; "he's runnin' like a turpentined cat"; "he starts for hell and gone and forty miles beyond" (more of his typical exaggeration). A similar exaggeration was the expression, "he run so fast that when he finally stopped it took his shadow forty minutes to ketch up with him." Forty seemed to be the cowboy's favorite number. One, telling of a companion getting away from a place in a hurry, said that "at the rate he's goin' you'd think he was packin' the mail"; and when another left in a hurry to avoid trouble, an observing cowboy commented, "When he saw the jackpot he was in he shore leaned forward and shoved."

Referring to some riders leaving town in a hurry to avoid a tangle with the law after having driven a herd of cattle to the shipping point, one of them said, "We lit a shuck without waitin' to kiss the mayor goodbye." Del Woods described another running upstairs to get away from a drunken cowboy "on the shoot" with, "He ran up them stairs like a rat up a rafter." A couple of expressions I have heard describing a slow horse in a race are: "He was as far behind the parade as a steam calliope," and "this other hoss left him like he was tied to a post." A high compliment to pay either man or horse was to say that "he could run like a Neuches steer."

Some expressions for commands to go included: "punch the breeze"; "hit the breeze"; "pull your freight"; "pull your freight for the tules"; "light a shuck"; "rattle your hocks"; "amble"; "slope"; or "dust." When a cowhand was fired and ordered off the ranch it was said that "the boss told him to dig out his bedroll and drift"; while it was said of one who left of his own accord that "he pulled his picket pin and drifted."

An animal leaving in a hurry "rolled his tail"; "curled his tail"; "humped his tail at the shore end"; or "made a nine in his tail." "Takin' to the tall timber" is another such expression. A person taking ordinary leave was apt to say, "Well, I got to be weavin' 'long"; and when the foreman ordered the cowhands to go on a hurried trip he might say: "Tie your hats to the saddle and let's go."

The West is noted for its open hospitality. There are no signs spelling "welcome" on the door-mats. It is acted instead of made in signs. All men are welcome at the ranch, and no questions asked of them. The rustler can sit at the table alongside a preacher and get the same courteous treatment if he behaves himself. It is a western law lived up to more than any law made in the courts. Quite often a man dropping in on some line-camp is, as one cowhand put it, "as welcome as a pardon to a lifer." Riding line is a lonesome life and Panhandle Colter, while performing this duty for the winter, once said that "every visitor was as welcome as an invitation to split a quart."

According to the western code you have to feed and shelter your worst enemy if he comes in a storm. If he spreads the news that you refused him you had better leave the country. Pack Mears was doing his best to spread such news when he said of a certain outfit, "You was welcome at that spread if you was on one of those visits where you just stand awhile with your hat in your hand, but they shore let you know you wouldn't be welcome to stay till the grub's all gone."

There are some individuals who never seem to be welcome anywhere. I have heard cowboys use such expressions in describing these folks as: "He's as welcome as a polecat at a picnic," and "he's welcome as a rattler in a dogtown"; and Mouthy Wells referred to such a man as being "about as welcome as a tax collector." When one met this breed he was "usually as polite to him as one strange bulldog to another," or, as Latigo Tate once put it, "We're about as polite to this jigger as a hound dog to a stray pup after his bone."

In glancing through my notes I find such expressions as: "He's as popular as a wet dog at a parlor social"; "he's as unpopular as a bear in a hog pen"; and of one who had overstayed his welcome Tod Myers said, "His cinch was gettin' frayed." Another spoke of an uncongenial guest as being "as sociable as an ulcerated tooth."

There were many close friendships on the range. About the oldest laws of the West were that you must not give away a friend; must not sell him out. One of the cowboy's oldest beliefs is that friendship did not mean much when a man was riding high, wide and handsome. It was when he was being trampled upon that counted. I have heard many friendships referred to with such expressions as: "Those fellers are gettin' 'long like two pups in a basket"; "they get 'long like two shoats in the same pigpen"; "they get 'long as peaceful as two six-guns in the same belt"; and "there's no more trouble between them than between a kitten and a warm brick."

If a cowboy really liked you "he'd go to the end of the trail for you"; "he'll stick to you as long as there's a button on Job's coat"; "he'd follow right up to hell's hottest backlog"; "he'd stay with you till the hens have the toothache" or "until Sittin' Bull stands up"; or "Hell will be a glacier before he'll quit you."

Bud Peters once spoke of such a friendship and declared, "Those two waddies are shore made of the same leather." Another said of two friends that "they're close 'nough to use the same toothpick." When Dud Russell told of the harmony at a certain ranch, he said, "Life on that spread ran as smooth as long sweetenin'." I have also heard close friendships between various ranch hands spoken of with such terms as: "They were thick as cloves on a Christmas ham"; "they were thick as hossflies in May"; "they were as thick as feathers in a pillow"; "they were thick as seven men on a cot"; "they were thick as hoss thieves in hell'; and "those two fellers were thicker'n splatter."

A true friend would "stick to you till they're cuttin' ice in Death Valley," and a sticker in a fight would "fight you till hell froze over then skate with you on the ice," or "he'd stick to you like death to a dead nigger." A deputy once told of chasing a rustler with, "I hung on his trail till he got saddle sores."

There are men with enemies and dislikes too, and Frosty Ferguson referred to such a man with the comment, "I ain't got no more use for him than I have a temperance lecturer." Hugh Floyd expressed like sentiments when he said, "I wouldn't speak to him if I met him in hell packin' a lump of ice on his head." Slash Curry once stated that an enemy had been "packin' that grudge against me as far back as an Injun could remember." Another rider told a yarn about two enemy ranchers in the course of which he stated that "when those two old alkalies met there was shore hair in the butter," meaning that this meeting created a delicate situation. Clint Davidson told of two old enemies that "got 'long like two bob-cats in a gunny sack."

The cowboy is a great admirer of beauty in anything, but in expressing his sentiments about the opposite sex he is usually too timid to declare himself except to his fellow workers. Around different campfires I have heard rough, bearded riders give voice to their admiration of some female with such expressions as: "She's as pretty as a red heifer in a flower bed"; "she's as soft and pretty as a young calf's ears"; "she's prettier'n a spotted pup under a red wagon"; and "she's prettier'n a chestnut filly." Other expressions of beauty they have been known to use are: "Pretty as a painted wagon"; "pretty as a heart flush"; "pretty as a basket of chips"; and "pretty as a cactus flower." One cowhand, in speaking of the good disposition of a lady friend, declared she was "as sweet and mild as barnyard milk."

A cowman might describe a good-looking man as "handsome as an ace-full on kings"; "he's handsome as a new stake rope on a thirty-dollar pony"; and I believe it was Silk Kutner who, upon meeting a duded-up tender-foot, remarked, "He's so pretty I feel like takin' off my hat ever'time I meet him."

"As ugly as galvanized sin," pretty well expresses the cowman's idea of lack of beauty, but he has many other expressions along this line too. Only on very few occasions have I heard a cowman speak disrespectfully of women. In speaking of a homely woman, he sometimes refers to her as a "Montgomery Ward woman sent West on approval," but he usually keeps his opinions to himself. One might occasionally hear some such description as "she's uglier'n a Mexican sheep," or "she's uglier'n a new sheared sheep."

Squint Higgins spoke of a certain man as being "so ugly the flies wouldn't light on him"; and Chet Savage described a man with a very low forehead by his graphic comment that "there wasn't 'nough room between his eyebrows and his hair to itch." Slack Rosser gave a physical description of a homely man by saying, "His front teeth stuck out so far he could eat popcorn out of a jug"; while another puncher said of a long-faced man that "he could eat oats out of a churn"; and that another "had a face as long as a dried possum hide." A lack of beauty might also be described as "ugly as a tar bucket," or "ugly as hammered mud."

If a cowboy attempted to describe a group of people who were in a happy frame of mind he would probably say they "were happy as a bunch of free niggers." Andy Kitchell, a young puncher in Arizona, once described a happy man as being "as chipper as a coopful of catbirds"; and Toad Preston, an old man in Montana, described the same condition by saying, "He's happier'n a lost soul in hell in a flood." Many expressions are in my notebooks such as: "Happy as a flea in a doghouse"; "happy as a heifer with a new fencepost"; "happy as a city kid in a peach orchard"; "happy as a pig in a peach orchard"; "happy as a little dog with two tails"; "happy as a dead pig in the sunshine"; or "happy as a pet parrot."

Another cowboy, during a trip to town with a month's pay in his Levi's, declared: "I'm enjoyin' life as much as a kid does pullin' a pup's ears." On one occasion, after the last cow had been prodded into the stock cars at the shipping pen and the crew had made their way to a saloon to wash the alkali from their throats, Kip Bronson described the bunch as being "as pleased as a bear cub with a new honeycomb." Years later in a western cowtown with my friend Cleve Mulhall, we walked down the street and ran into a mutual friend. When he saw us a happy grin spread over his face, and Cleve, in his characteristic cowboy style, said: "Look at that old sagecock. I reckon

he's glad to see us, he's grinnin' like a skunk eatin' garlic."
I have also heard the expression "grinnin' like a cat eatin'
liver."

Cochise Jones once spoke of a man being "so light-
hearted he's liftin' his feet like a sandhill crane walkin'
up a river bed"; and Frijole Holt told of another who had
heard some good news that made him "go off steppin' as
high as a blind dog in a wheatfield." Another described
a well-pleased person as "purrin' like a tomcat in a
creamery"; and one who had heard good news was
described with, "His spirits rose like a cob in a cistern."

On the other hand, the cowman may speak of an
unhappy person as being "sad as a bloodhound's eye";
"happy as a hog bein' dragged away from a feed trough";
or speak of an individual as "his luck's runnin' kinda
muddy." To a cowboy a person all "buggered up" with
misery or sadness might "look like a motherless calf," or
"look like a throwout from a footsore remuda." He might
"look as sad as a tick-fevered dogie," or "look so bad his
ears flop." Soggy Reid once said, "I got some news that
shore swiped the silver linin' off my cloud, and left me
about as happy as a duck in Arizona." Another expressed
the same thought with the comment, "I'm about as happy
as a duck waitin' for rain in Arizona."

I heard a weather-beaten puncher, in telling of an
incident that touched his heart, say, "I didn't shed no
tears but I damned near choked to death." At another
time when someone told a touching story, a tenderhearted
cowboy, brushing away a tear he was trying to hide, said,
"The smoke of your campfire got in my eyes."

Pony Teal told of a man who "looked as melancholy
as a hound settin' on the doorstep of a deserted cabin";
and Jim Houston mentioned another as "sufferin' like a
centipede with the sciatic rheumatism." A man who
always seemed to be in trouble was said to "have more

troubles than Job had boils." I have heard many unique cowboy descriptions of someone sad, such as: "His lip's hangin' down like a blacksmith's apron"; "his lip's hangin' as limp as the dewlap on a dogie's brisket"; "his lip's stickin' out like a buggy seat"; and "he had about as much fun as a baby with the bellyache."

A wise person was said to be "as wise as a tree full of owls," or "as wise as a pack rat." Sam Fletcher, in telling of the wagon cook's knowledge concerning digging out bullets from one's wound, stated, "Cookie knew more about such things than a squaw does about crackin' cooties on a papoose's foretop." A smart person was said to be "smart as a cuttin' hoss"; "smart 'nough to be Justice of the Peace"; or "smart as a bunkhouse rat." And when speaking of a well-educated man, I heard one cowhand say, "He's educated to a feather edge." Another spoke of such a man as "upholstered with more brains than a sheep dog," and still another expressed the same thought with, "He's as full of information as a mail-order catalog." Other expressions along this subject I have gathered are: "He's as long-headed as a mule"; "a pet fox is plumb foolish alongside of him"; and "he's a regular chaparral fox." One described a smart lawyer he knew as "the greatest law giver since Moses," and another informed me that "he don't need advice any more'n a steer needs a saddle blanket." Posthole Farley claimed his boss "knew more about the cow business than a rabbit does about runnin'."

On the other hand, ignorance is one thing with which the cowman has little patience, and his speech referring to this quality is rather vicious. In speaking of such a man Cactus Shindler once said that "he don't know enough to pack guts to a bear." In Texas I heard an ignorant man referred to as being "as shy of brains as a terrapin is of feathers"; and in New Mexico Bobby Blair spoke of a man whose "brain cavity wouldn't make a drinkin' cup for a hummin' bird."

Dusty Lynch said of such a man that "he's got no more sense than a little nigger with a big navel"; and far away in another state I heard a cowboy express the same thought with, "He ain't got no more brains than a Chihuahua dog has hair." An ignorant person to one cowboy "couldn't drive nails in a snow bank"; to another he might be "as chuckle-headed as a prairie dog"; to another "he didn't have nothin' under his hat but hair"; while another just bluntly expressed his opinion with the terse remark, "His thinker's puny."

Soapy Riley stated his opinion of a mentally weak man by saying, "If his brains was assayed they wouldn't show half an ounce of idea to the ton"; and at a later date I heard Peewee Simms express a like opinion with the comment that "all he knows about brains is that you can buy 'em with scrambled eggs." "He don't know no more about it than a hog does a ruffled shirt," was Jase Bunton's way of speaking of a lack of knowledge a fellow rider showed about a certain subject; and another puncher uttered a like description with, "He don't know as much about it as a hog does a sidesaddle." Other phrases one might hear on the range are: "He knew about as much about it as a hog does a hip pocket in a bathin' suit," or "he didn't know any more about such things than a hog knows about sin."

The tenderfoot is not expected to be wise in the ways of cattle-land, but the most inexcusable ignorance is when he "can't tell the Injun side of a hoss," which, as you likely know, is the right side and the opposite side from which the white man mounts. Stumpy Donnelly, in speaking of a certain tenderfoot, said, "He can't tell skunks from house cats and needs a wet nurse." Whimpy Jones contended that "none of 'em knowed sic 'em."

The cowboy has many ways of expressing his idea of someone being crazy. Jotted down in my notebooks are such phrases as "he's crazier'n a locoed bedbug"; "crazy as a sheepherder"; "crazy as a woman's watch"; "crazy as popcorn on a hot stove"; "crazy as a milk cow"; and from Dusty Lynch, speaking of me and of my collecting this lingo, "crazy as a parrot eatin' sticky candy." Blackie Boyd spoke of one such as being "so feather-headed his memory's pulled its picket-pin," while another puncher referred to such a person with, "He's off his mental reservation." Cy Little spoke of one whose "memory's as dim as the old buffalo trails"; and I have heard other such expressions as "the Lord poured in his brains with a teaspoon and somebody jiggled His arm"; "his head's so hollow he's got to talk with his hands to get away from the echo"; "he's stronger in the back than he is north of the ears"; "his intelligence ain't in camp"; "if you bored a hole in his head you wouldn't find 'nough brains to grease a gimlet"; and "he couldn't sell hacksaws in a hoosgow." If the one spoken of was childlishly foolish it might be said that "he ought to be playin' with a string of spools." I heard one cowboy say of another that "he's studyin' to be a half-wit, but I'm afraid he won't make the grade."

Other expressions depicting ignorance I have heard at various ranches include: "He couldn't teach a settin' hen to cluck"; "he didn't know where-at to scratch a hog"; "he didn't know cactus when he was settin' on it"; and one cowhand spoke of another as "so narrow-minded he could look through a knothole with both eyes at once."

One also met some undiscerning characters on the range and I have heard the cowman use such expressions to describe them as: "He couldn't see through a ladder," and "he couldn't see through a bob-wire fence"; or, as Snag Welch said, "He's blind as a snubbin' post." Nig Pepper once remarked, "He's blind as a rattler in

August"; and another said that "he's blind as a steeple bat."

Whatever else could be said of the cowboy he had "sand in his craw"; and in speaking of a brave man the speaker was likely to say that "he's got more sand than the Mojave Desert," or was "gritty as fish eggs rolled in sand"; "his craw was jammed plumb full of sand and fightin' tallow"; "he had plenty of gravel in his gizzard"; "he had 'nough sand for a lake front"; or "he had more guts than you could hang on a fence."

Of a courageous man in a gun fight, one might describe him as being "as calm as a toad in the sun," or "as cool as a skunk in the moonlight." A man always ready for a fight would "fight a rattler and give him first bite," or "fight a circle saw and give it three revolutions." Some would-be badman, said Tod Nelson, "chargin' 'round as free and fearless as a cyclone, didn't scare nobody with bones in his spinal column because a brave man knew how to die standin' up."

Anyone not possessing these qualities had small place in the cowboy's life. He who "ran his boot heels over side-steppin' trouble" was said to "have a yellow streak down his back so wide it lapped plumb around to his brisket bone," or was "yellow as a dandelion"; "as yellow as mustard without the bite"; and might be advised to "hunt up somethin' you can use for a backbone." Such a person's "guts had turned to fiddle strings," or it was said that "he didn't have any more guts than a snake has hips," and "you could take a bunch of corn cobs and lightnin' bugs and make him run till his tongue hung out like a calf rope."

One afraid of guns might be said to be "as gun-shy as a female institute." "He's as scared as a rabbit in a wolf's mouth," or "he's paper-backed and built of butter," are other expressions I have heard concerning cowards.

One cowhand speaking of a coward he had run across in the desert country, said that "he shore had cold feet for such a hot country." Old man Colville told of one such with, "He ran a bunch of Comanches nearly to death, but he was in the lead." In such a "cold-footed" person, as one cowboy commented, "There's no more harm in him than in a chambermaid." Of one exceedingly frightened it was said that "he's shakin' like a willow in the wind"; and as one cowhand said, "It wouldn't take no jag of lead to make him hit the trail."

Though the average cowhand was not afraid of man, there were times when he did not mind admitting his fear of the supernatural and of the action of nature's elements, such as a fierce lightning storm or a tornado. One admitted that "by the feelin' that's runnin' up and down my spine, if I'd a-had bristles I'd resembled a wild hog," while another admitted that such an experience "made his skin get up and crawl all over me with cold feet"; and still another, in speaking of a night when the lightning was playing on the horses' ears and the cattle's horns, displaying balls of fire, said, "It'd make the hair on a buffalo robe stand up."

The cowman's life is full of danger and he thinks little of such things. I have heard very few expressions on this subject. However, I did hear a puncher, in speaking of a certain gunman, advise that "crossin' that killer's as dangerous as walkin' in quicksand over hell." Whimpy Jones once told a yarn about a friend who had a close call and he ended by saying, "After all the danger was over he heaved such a sigh you could feel the draft." One cowboy told of his own experience with, "When I looked into the danger end of that scatter-gun it didn't take me long to pull in my horns." Another, in telling of an experience he had had, said, "When I see the fix I'm in I started askin' old St. Peter for a passport." Still another, telling of a friend in trouble with the law, commented, "That was one tight he couldn't come out of with all his tail feathers." A dangerous situation, as one cowhand said, could be "dangerous as bein' up the same saplin' with a cinnamon bear"; or some situation might be "as risky as braidin' a mule's tail."

The cowboy's expression for harmlessness may be such as, "He's harmless as a pet rabbit." Flint Lawther once spoke contemptuously of another with, "He makes big talk, but there's no more harm in him than in a new-born babe"; and Nick Pelster, in one of his yarns, said that "when he got the bulge" on a would-be badman, the latter "was mild as the month of May." Swing Harper once referred to someone as being "helpless as a cow in quicksand"; and Pokey Olsen spoke of another being "helpless as a frozen snake"; while another expressed the same thought with, "He's as harmless as a bull snake."

The cowboy also has his expressions for peacefulness. To mention a few, I recall such phrases as: "He's peaceful as a church"; "he's serene as a prayer meetin'"; "he's as peaceful as a thumb in a baby's mouth"; and I once heard Skeet Nelson remark that the weather was "as calm and peaceful as a hoss trough."

Chuck Evans once spoke of an old-timer as being "so obstinate he wouldn't move camp for a prairie fire"; and at another time, in speaking of an Arizona ranch owner, Billy Gordon said, "The old man's as obstinate as a cow with a suckin' calf."

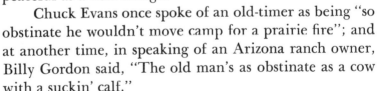

## Assorted Figures of Speech

IT IS SAID of a worthless person that "he ain't worth a barrel of shucks"; "he ain't fit to shoot at when you want to unload and clean your gun"; "his family tree was a scrub"; or "he was onery as a corn-drunk squaw." Anyone who could not be trusted might be described as being "as unreliable as a woman's watch." He might be someone whom he "wouldn't trust as far as I could throw an elephant against the wind." Jinks Palmer expressed the same thought with, "I wouldn't trust him as far as I could throw a posthole." A man might also be "one of those guys you wouldn't dare to sleep alongside of with your mouth open if you had a gold tooth."

A useless object was said to be "as useless as a .22 cartridge in an eight-gauge shotgun"; "as useless as a hymn book to a rustler"; "as useless as four-card flush"; or "as useless as teats on a boar hog." One cowhand expressed the same thought when he described an object which he did not need or want with, "I've got 'bout as much use for that as a bull has teats"; and another, in a similar vein, said, "I've got no more use for that than Noah had for a tail light on his ark." Snuffles Hill's idea of something useless was to be "as useless as a knot in a stake rope."

Brick Hancock, describing a difficult job he had, said, "It was like tyin' down a bobcat with a shoestring," and I heard another speak of the difficulty of finding something with, "It was as hard to find as a fly in a currant pie." The idea of trouble might be expressed with such idioms as "he had more trouble than a one-armed man with the 'dobe itch," or "he had more trouble than a harelipped man tryin' to whistle."

The cowman also had many expressions to describe his idea of trying to accomplish the impossible, such as: "It was like tryin' to scratch your ear with your elbow"; "you might as well been barkin' at a knot"; "like an elephant tryin' to use a typewriter"; or "as easy as trimmin' the whiskers off the man in the moon." When he believed he had little chance of finding a hunted object he would perhaps say that he "might as well try to find hair on a frog"; or "he might as well hunt for a hossthief in Heaven." If it was a contest, be it a fight or a frolic, where he had small chance of winning, he was said to "have as much chance as a wax cat in hell." Other such expressions heard include: "He had about as much chance as a grasshopper that hops into an anthill"; "he didn't have no more chance than an Easter egg in an orphanage"; "didn't have no more show than a hen at a mass-meetin' of coyotes"; "didn't have no more show than a one-legged man in a kickin' contest"; or "didn't have as much chance as a pack rat at a coyote convention."

Something hard to find was "like huntin' for a whisper in a big wind." One cowboy, describing his failure to win an argument, said that "it was like arguin' with the shadow of death"; and another said his argument "didn't have no more effect than pourin' water on a drowned rat." Yet another, telling of an argument he had against a raise in taxes, said his talk "had about as much influence as a steer on a calf crop." I have also heard the expression that "he couldn't get as far as I could throw a bull by the tail," in speaking of the impossibility of an escape.

On the other hand, something easily accomplished had an equal number of expressions, such as: "It was as easy as guttin' a slut"; "as easy as eatin' striped candy"; "as easy as robbin' a bird's nest"; "as easy as a hoss' tail ketchin cockle-burs"; "as easy as a kitten hoppin' over a caterpillar"; "as easy as a hossfly ridin' a mule's ear"; "as easy as shootin' fish in a barrel"; "as easy as throwin' a two-day old calf"; and "as easy as lickin' butter off a knife." I have also heard something described as being "as free and easy as suicide." "That's a hoss easy curried," tells of a task easily accomplished; or to another it might be "as simple as a primer."

Most cowboys, especially the younger ones, are restless to a certain extent. They want to see what is over the next hill and do not settle down long in one place. A cowboy considers his home to be "where he spreads his blanket." Tin-Cup Davis used to say, after he had stayed on a ranch for what he considered a long time, "I've been here so long the rust's beginnin' to flake off of me."

Ham Cordray described a bunch of reckless riders as "ridin' 'round like hornets in a bonnet." Deuce McQuirk spoke of a restless friend as "wanderin' 'round like a pony with the bridle off," and Jake Lane described another as "movin' 'round like a hen on a hot griddle." Chub Davis, who had wandered over the whole West, argued against marrying and settling down by saying, "I want to wear out a couple more saddles before I pick me a corral." Restlessness has also been depicted as "he's homeless as a poker chip"; "he'd rather leave his hide on a fence than stay in the corral"; "he's always fightin' the bits till he gets on the trail that leads to some other place"; and "he's like a loose hoss full of cockle-burs, and always lookin' for new pastures." Restless cattle were said to be "junin' 'round"; and one night rider, describing a bedded-down herd when a storm was approaching, said, "Them steers were so restless you'd have to ride a mile to spit."

Paint Parker, whom I met in my wanderings, was noted for his frequent changes of location and his restlessness. In discussing these qualities I once heard another cowhand remark that "Paint had so much iron in his system that if he hung 'round one place long he'd rust," but I later learned he was trying to stay "two steps ahead of the sheriff."

The cowboy was always hungry. The outdoor work he did built up an appetite so large "his belly always felt as empty as the Grand Canyon." If he had to postpone a few meals in the performance of his duty he never complained, but perhaps later told about the time when his "stomach was so shrunk it wouldn't hold a liver pill." Whizzer Grimes once told of an occasion when he was "hungry 'nough to eat a saddle blanket," and others have said that "I'm hungry 'nough to eat mutton with the wool still on"; or, "I could eat a folded tarp."

I was walking down the street in Tucson one day with a couple of cowhands when one of them said, "Let's go down to that chili joint on the corner and get a bowl of red. I'm hungrier'n a woodpecker with the headache." The other agreed. "That's fine with me. My tapeworm's shore hollerin' for fodder." A cowboy in Texas remarked that "I'm so hungry I could eat a sow and nine pigs and chase the boar half a mile"; and another similarly expressed his hunger after a funeral he had attended with, "I'm so hungry I could've eaten the corpse and chased the mourners to the graveyard."

Smokey Kerley, telling of an extended fast he was compelled to take, added, "My empty paunch was a-rattlin' till I was plumb gut-shrunk." Another rider, after being on the trail and going without food for some time, said, "Before I got back I was shore narrow at the equator." Buzz Carson, relating his experiences with a diet of salt pork, explained that "I was so saturated with hog fat I sweated straight leaf lard and my hide got so slick I could hardly keep my clothes on"; and Flint Lawther told of a similar experience by saying, "I et so much hog belly I grunted in my sleep and was afraid to look for fear I'd sprouted a curly tail." Another said he "got damned tired of eatin' pig's vest with buttons."

One cowboy described another eating a hearty meal, by saying "he was shore paddin' out his belly." Another told of a time he was in town and visited the boss of the ranch. He was asked to stay for dinner and later said, "There was so much grub I wondered how I was goin' to eat my way out." One who had been out of work for some time commented wistfully, "I'd shore like to grease my chin again with a good steak."

The wagon boss informed the cook that we were going to have visitors by telling him, "Put your best foot in the soup, Cookie, there's goin' to be company for supper." I heard one of the boys criticize this same cook's cooking with the comment, "Old Coosie just bogs down some raisins in dough and calls her puddin'." Not all wagon cooks were good ones and at times the cowboy had a right to complain, as one did, about the tough meat he was served, with, "This beef acts like it was sawed right off the horns of some old range bull. You can hardly dish the gravy out with a fork." "Talk about your cut straw and molasses," said Matt Rogers. "That wagon dished up the sorriest grub I ever et."

One old-timer claimed he "never had indigestion but once in my life and that was when somebody slipped mutton in my stew while in town one day." The early-day cowman had little use for sheep and the men who herded them. Any person "who favored mutton instead of beef" was a "low man on the totem pole." There is an old saying that "a sheepherder's always got a grouch and a Waterbury watch, and when he ain't a-nursin' the one he's a-windin' the other." One cowboy I talked to stated, "There ain't nothin' dumber than sheep except the man who herds 'em." Jesse Lane, speaking of a certain cattle range, once said, "That range is so against sheep I wouldn't ride through it with a wool shirt on."

A cowhand described an Englishman drinking his tea at a hotel in town, by saying, "He supped that tea like it was hot solder." Describing the food served at a dance at the YO Ranch, Dobe Miller said of the hostess, "She's got cakes and pies, fluff-duffs and other throat-ticklin' grub just to remind the boys they ain't eatin' at the wagon." Often when on the trail the cook had to use very muddy water for his cooking. One cowboy described such water as "water thick 'nough to plow," and I've heard such expressions as "the river was so muddy the cook's bread was soggy," and "the water was so thick you couldn't drink it, but it wasn't quite thick 'nough to eat with a fork." Another said, "That water was so thick you had to use sandpaper to get the settlin's out of your mouth."

Bob Ellis, speaking of a friend who had squatted on a certain range, commented, "If he ran low on his own cut of bacon he'd ride the chuck-line." A great many of the old range cooks were ex-punchers too stove-up to ride, but a lot of them were men who "didn't savvy cow unless it was dished up in a stew." As long as they kept a pot of strong coffee on the fire they could get away with murder. Every cowhand is a fool about his coffee. Like his liquor, he wants it straight and strong, "strong 'nough to float a wedge." As Sam Haywood used to say, "Gimme a cup of coffee that'll kick up in the middle and pack double."

Every visitor, when he approaches headquarters, a line-camp or the wagon, is made welcome with such cowman invitations as: "Climb down and eat a bean"; "crawl off and cool your saddle"; "fall off and feed your tapeworm"; "hang your hoss on the fence and turn your saddle out to graze"; or "the beans are a-bilin', come in and put your feet under the table."

You have perhaps seen a cow start running from a sort of crouch. One cowhand described this with, "That cow come out of the corral a-stoopin'." Another, in describing a steer which broke out of a pen, said, "That steer walks through that fence like a fallin' tree through cobwebs." Telling of a time he was on night guard after the herd had been bedded down, another cowboy remarked that "there's always some old stampeder a-layin' out on the edge of the herd lookin' for boogers."

In discussions of the difference between range cattle and the domestic kind, I've heard such remarks as that "them's the kind of cows you could move up on with a stool and a bucket"; or as one said, "Them hornless critters that wear bells and are punched with a stool." In referring to the range variety the cowman might say, "Them cows ain't never been handled by milk-maids."

When a cowhand wanted to express his opinion of someone conceited, he might use such terms as: "He's as full of conceit as a barber's cat"; "he's conceited as a flea full of blood"; or "he's one of them fellers that thinks the sun comes up 'specially to hear him crow." Another said of such a person that "his head's swelled up as big as a kraut barrel."

To the cowhand something empty was "empty as a gutted steer"; "empty as a burned-out lantern"; or "bare and dry as a farmer's feed lot." One cowhand, speaking of the range where not an animal was in sight, said, "The whole range is as empty as a church."

I have heard uncomfortable situations described as "uncomfortable as a hoss thief at a hangin' bee"; "as uncomfortable as a camel in the Klondyke"; or "as uncomfortable as ridin' night herd in the rain without a slicker." Anything solemn to a cowboy might be "as solemn as a tenderfoot trapper skinnin' a skunk"; "as solemn as a tree full of owls"; "as solemn as soap"; or "as solemn as Moses."

Like everything else in the cowboy's life, his idea of helplessness is described with some unique expressions. I have heard such idioms as "helpless as a cow in quicksand"; "helpless as a frozen snake"; "helpless as a dummy with his hands cut off"; and "helpless as a worm in a bed of ants." A tired person might be "as tired as a bull cat after an all night prowl in the mud." Something soft might be expressed as "soft as a goose-hair pillow," or "soft as bear grease."

Anything so noticeable that it assumes prominence is apt to be spoken of in such terms as "plain as paint"; "plain as the hump on a camel"; "plain as the ears on a mule"; "plain as the horn on a saddle"; or "plain as plowed ground." Concho Bates once spoke of a man dressed in an outfit that made him "prominent as a zebra"; and Hondo O'Dell, speaking of an Eastern dude, declared that he looked "as prominent as a new saloon in a church district"; while another cowhand once referred to a certain object that "showed up like a tin roof in a fog." "As plain as an Injun signboard" (a bleached shoulder bone of a buffalo upon which Indians painted signs) was another common expression. On one occasion I heard a cowhand describe something as being "as prominent as a boil on a pug nose," and another described something as being "as plain as a shirt tail on a stick."

The cowboy has his own ideas of a polite person and is apt to say that "he was as polite as a barber"; "polite as a whipped nigger"; "polite as a tinhorn gambler on pay-day"; or "polite as a colored preacher talkin' to the devil." I heard one cowboy describe such a person as "bowin' and bendin' like a pig over a nut." Anyone who has seen a pig trying to eat a hickory nut will find this an apt description.

The cowman has also invented some expressions to convey his idea of surprise or of something unexpected, such as Carter Johnson who described someone so surprised that "he looked like somebody had showed him four aces and a joker in a big jackpot." Hap Frey spoke of another cowhand being "as surprised as a dog with his first porcupine." Another puncher, in describing a fight, said of one of the fighters, "His next move was as unexpected as a fifth ace in a poker deck." "It was as unexpected as a rattlesnake in your bedroll," and "it was as unexpected as gun play in a Bible class," are other figures of speech I have heard on the range.

Very few of the old dyed-in-the-wool cowboys wanted to live in town. They would have felt "as out of place as a cow on a front porch." One old-timer who had returned to the ranch from the city where he had gone to visit his daughter was asked how he liked town life.

"You couldn't hold me in one of those places with a Spanish bit," he answered. "Give me a country where a man can switch his tail."

The early-day cowtowns were wild and woolly, and as Bullfoot Grimes said of one, "She's shore a town with the hair on." Such a town, in the words of Rawhide Gilson "would be a bad place to have your gun stick." Usually the streets were lined with saloons, and one cowman observed that "it's a town where most of the doors swing both ways." One cowboy who had spent some time in a town near the Mexican border described it as "a town of sand, sun and siestas." Another, describing a dance hall in an Arizona town, said, "In that dance hall the gals bared more hide to the evenin' breeze than an Injun in a breech clout." Another cowhand described a town where killings were frequent by saying that "it was one of those tough towns where the undertaker was the most prosperous man in it."

Turkey Red (a nickname shortened from Turkey Track Red and given to distinguish him from the other redheads of the immediate range) had never been to a large town until the boss sent him to Fort Worth with a load of steers. After checking in the cattle at the stockyards in North Fort Worth, he decided to catch a streetcar and put up in Fort Worth proper so he could see the sights.

All his life he had heard about smooth city-slickers so he was wary. After he had registered at the hotel, one of the bellhops picked up his luggage to lead him to the elevator.

"They call them fellers bellhops," said Turkey Red in telling of his trip. "I didn't see no bells on 'em, but I shore made one of 'em hop. This hopper picks up my warbag like he's goin' to take it away some place. I didn't figger to lose that sack of my savin's of a lifetime. All my low-necked clothes and my pet six-gun was in that sack.

"I tried to grab it away from him, but he hangs onto it like an Injun to a whisky jug and grins like a jackass eatin' cactus. This make me mad 'nough to kick a hog barefooted so I digs my boot heel into his toes and bears down like I'm ropin' a bronc on foot.

"Well, sir, this hombre not only lets go all holts, but he lets loose a howl that'd make a she-wolf jealous and starts jumpin' up and down like a barrel boundin' down hill. For a while he looks busier'n a little dog in high oats."

Turkey Red might not have known "sic 'em" about city life, but I defy the most educated city man to tell of such an experience in a more forceful or picturesque language.

When a cowhand gets the "saddle itch" and wants to see what is on the other side of the hill, he wants to stay in the cow country and be with his own kind. Only occasionally would one "pull his picket pin" or "slip his hobbles" to drift East, as one would say, "to have his horns knocked off," or "get the hay out of his horns." But as Bud Lucas used to say about the cowboy's travels, "Goin' 'round a coffee pot huntin' for the handle would cover the extent of his travels."

One cowhand was bragging about the places he had been when one of the other riders shut him up with, "When you hit this ranch you was so green we had to tie your foot up to give you a haircut. I know for a fact that you've never been closer to the risin' sun than the Pecos River."

When one is energetic and keeps busy he may be described as, in the words of Swing Harper, "busy as a one-armed man saddlin' a green bronc," or as Tex Roper put it, "busy as a sackful of wildcats." Other such expressions in my notebooks are: "busier'n a hen drinkin' a can of paint"; "he's busier'n a one-armed monkey at a flea festival"; "busy as hell beatin' tanbark"; "busier'n a brockle-faced dogie in flytime"; "busy as a tumblebug in a mule track"; "as busy as a bee in a tarbucket"; and "busy as a bartender on Saturday night."

Laziness is commonly described in such apt phrases as "lazy 'nough to be a good fiddler"; "lazy as a hound dog in the sun"; "so lazy molasses wouldn't run down his legs"; and Wishbone Wilson spoke of one being "so lazy he has to lean against a buildin' to spit." Jesse Thorp once expressed his opinion of a lazy man with, "He keeps about as busy as a hibernatin' bear."

Curly Hicks told of a lazy person by saying, "He didn't do nothin' but set 'round all day on his one spot," and another expressed the same thought by saying that "he was always settin' on his end gate." Rocky Rhodes had the same idea when he spoke of one "settin' on the south side of his pants." Of another, Hank Bowden observed, "The hardest work he ever done was to take a long squint at the sun and a quick squat in the shade." When Tom Sutter got a new job and was put to digging postholes, he quit and "allowed he wouldn't be caught on the blister end of *no* damned shovel." A lazy man was also said to be "lazy as a chilled rattler," or "too lazy to smile."

In describing bigness the cowman has been heard to refer to some object as being "bigger'n an eight-mule baggage wagon," or "bigger'n a load of hay." Pronto Barnes told of a friend who had "put on so much tallow he's heavy as a dead bear." Another was described as being "so fat you'd have to throw a diamond hitch to keep him in the saddle"; and Zeb Fisher, in referring to a very large man, described him with, "For weight and size he'd take first prize at a bull show." Another cowhand described a big man as being "as wide as a barn door and long as a wagon track."

An old cowhand on the Spur Ranch, in speaking of a certain puncher with large feet, declared that "he had feet the size of a loadin' chute." Tug Naylor described another by saying, "Most of his weight's on the spur end," and another told of a fellow puncher having "feet so big his tracks looked like where a steer had bedded down." Rusty Pence, in describing a friend's large hands, declared that when this man's hand was placed upon an object, "it covered it like a carpet." To Cal Travis, when he saw his opponent's poker hand, "It showed up as big as a skinned hoss"; and to Bill Berkhofer something large was "big as a hoop on a molasses barrel."

A large space might be described as "big 'nough to bed down a night herd." One cowhand described a Mexican spur he had seen as being "big as a soup plate." Another, when he went into a city restaurant, ordered a steak "as big as a mule's lip from the ears down"; and a puncher who had just caught a cootie on his body, said "he was big as a yearlin' that's followed his mammy all winter." A similar expression is that "he was big 'nough to shade an elephant." And I once heard Buck Weaver speak of a room as being "so small you couldn't cuss a cat without gettin' fur in your mouth."

Noise, like everything else in the cowboy's life, came in for its slangy expressions. Homer Anderson spoke of a man "makin' more noise than a jackass in a tin barn"; Tonto Sutter told of one "makin' more noise than hell turned out for noon"; while in New Mexico Frank Chattey spoke of another "makin' more noise than an empty wagon on a frozen road"; and Curly Hicks described a certain meeting as being "noisy as a calf corral." Rocky Rhodes once referred to a stampede with, "It sounded like hell emigratin' on cart wheels"; and Duke Noel told of an occasion where there was so much noise "it sounded like hell on a holiday." When an angry cowboy was stomping around in the bunkhouse giving vent to his spleen, one cowhand remarked that "he was bargin' 'round like a moose in a wigwam."

Other descriptions of the cowboy's idea of noise have been expressed with such phrases as: "It sounded like a herd of long yearlin's in a brandin' pen"; "it's makin' so much noise it would give a boilermaker the jitters"; "it sounded like a Mexican revolution"; and "he's noisy as a hoss in a dance hall." Pony Teal once described something noisy with, "It made so much noise it made a brass band sound like a rattle-box"; and another spoke of someone making "so much noise it would drive a temperance lecturer to drink."

The cowboy had his expressions for quietness too, such as describing something as "quiet as a hossthief after a hangin'," and "quiet as a thief in a chicken house." Things could also be "as quiet as a sick cow in a snow storm," or the situation might be "as placid as a duck pond."

To one cowboy a person "all buggered up with misery" might "look like a motherless calf," or "look like a throwout from a footsore remuda." To another he might "look as sad as a tick-fevered dogie." Pony Teal told of a man who "looked as melancholy as a hound settin' on the doorstep of a deserted cabin," and Jim Houston mentioned another as "sufferin' like a centipede with the sciatic rheumatism."

During a depression when "times were so hard the buffalo on a nickel started losin' flesh," and "times were harder than a merchant's credit eye," Medicine Lang declared that, with the low prices of cattle and the lack of money in the country, he "was gettin' worried as a bullfrog waitin' for rain in Arizona." Wishbone Wilson on one occasion told of an old rancher who was so soured on life "he had about as much fun as a baby with the belly-ache," and "his lip was hangin' as limp as the dewlap on a dogie's brisket." When Stan Wheeler had some domestic trouble he declared "he had more trouble than Job had boils." And when Highline Ott went to see the boss on a matter of business, he came back with the news that "the old man's so glum you'd a-thought the tax collector was in town."

Poisonous snakes are a natural enemy of man, and a cowman will go out of his way to kill one, fearing that if he passes up such an opportunity it might live to strike a friend. Tom Kirk spoke of a snaky section where the "snakes were so thick there you'd have to parade 'round on stilts to keep from gettin' bit"; and I heard another describe a rattler with, "That's the biggest snake I ever saw without the aid of likker."

To an Easterner a black night might be merely "black as midnight," or some such mild phrase, but the Westerner again brings into play the strength of his metaphors with "black as a blacksmith's apron"; "dark as a black cat's overcoat"; "dark as the inside of a cow"; "dark as a stack of black cats"; "dark as a wolf's mouth"; "dark as a stovepipe"; or "dark as midnight under a skillet." I have often heard cowhands say that it was "so dark you couldn't find your nose with both hands." Matt Roland once declared, "The night's so black the bats all stayed home." "Black as a stack of stove lids," "black as a spade flush," and "black as a chuck wagon skillet," are other descriptive figures I have heard on the range.

In expressing his opinion of the slowness of a certain horse, an old puncher on the Wineglass snorted disgustedly that "he [the horse] runs like he was goin' uphill with hobbles on." On another occasion Snip Ross spoke of a horse as being "slow as a cow in a swamp." In referring to a certain man Jimmie Butler once stated that he was "slow as a snail climbin' a slick log," and of another that "he was too slow to grow fast." Of a man slow in action, Rig Curry once said, "It took him longer'n it'd take a can't-whistle [a hare-lipped person] to call a dog."

Another cowhand spoke of a fellow worker as being "so slow that if he laid down by the river to get a drink the weeds would grow over him"; and Ron Coolidge, speaking of another said that "he moves 'round like he's got hobbles on." Similar descriptions range from "he's so slow he couldn't stop quick," to "he's slow as a snail on crutches." One cowhand telling of his group traveling through a rough country said that "we was travelin' at a gait so slow it wouldn't tire a papoose"; and Tom Noyce described such a trip with, "We went slow and steady, like a tom cat eatin' on a grindstone."

Quickness, on the other hand, was often expressed with the one word "pronto." "First rattle out of the box" expressed prompt action, while "like the devil beatin' tanbark" meant fast and furious, and "from who laid the chunk" was an expression signifying action or quality in the superlative degree.

I have heard many phrases on the range that express the quickness with which things can happen, such as: "It didn't last as long as a drink of whisky"; "it didn't last as long as a rattlesnake in a cowboy's bootleg"; "it didn't last as long as two-bits in a poker game"; and "it didn't last as long as a white shirt in a bear fight." Posthole Farley, telling of the quickness of action, stated that "it all happened in less time than it'd take an old maid to crawl under a bed." Pike Delaney stated that he once left a certain place "quicker'n a stutterin' man could holler shucks." Another, speaking of a fight he was in, said, "I crawled that jigger's hump quicker'n hell could scorch a feather." Latigo Tate once told of a gun fight he was in and stated that his enemy "got the bulge on me before a flea could hop out of danger."

During my travels through the cattle country, I have heard various apt and amusing comments upon quickness which range from "quicker'n you could spit and holler howdy"; " quicker'n old St. Peter could slam the door in the face of a hossthief"; "quicker'n a coyote can smell a carcass"; "quicker'n you could down a drink"; to "quick as powder."

Describing a puncher, who, caught afoot in the corral with a mad cow, barely saved himself by an alert, incredible leap for the top rail of the fence, his witnesses said that "he shore 'nough flea-hopped for them rails." It was said of one with the ability for quick action that "he was plenty nimble-blooded." Another cowhand, telling of a companion who had suddenly left the group in a hurry, said, "He quit us like a scorpion had crawled down his neck." Another expressed the same thought when he remarked that "they hopped away from there like a bunch of tree frogs." "Lightnin' hangs fire by comparison" is another way the cowman might express quickness; and something quickly consumed "wouldn't last as long as a keg of cider at a barn raisin'," or "wouldn't last as long as a grasshopper in a chicken yard." It might be said of anyone trying to leave a group without attracting attention that "he began to fade out like an old maid at a mothers' convention." Or, if one left in a hurry for a trip to town, someone might observe that "he heads for town like a coyote for a campfire." One who was quick in his actions might be described as "lively as a lobo with a knot in his tail." If a group suddenly dispersed, it might be said that "they scattered like a bunch of snowbirds."

# More Figures of Speech

THE COWBOY WORKS in all kinds of weather and his experiences make him apt in describing the various kinds he encounters. In extremely cold weather Soapy Riley used to rant about it being "colder than the knob of the North Pole," and Pony Teal used to say, "It was colder than hell on the stoker's holiday." I once heard another puncher speak of "ridin' in weather that'd make a polar bear hunt cover"; and Spade Wilson, who had formerly worked around Amarillo, Texas, declared that "when them Texas northers just poured off the North Pole there was nothin' to stop 'em but a bob-wire fence and it was full of knot-holes."

Another might express his opinion of the weather as being "as sodden and cold as a clay farm in the month of

March." Other equally graphic idioms on the subject are: "It's colder than a well-digger in Montana"; "it's colder'n a well-chain in December"; and "it's as cold as Christmas in Amarillo." "Cold as a clam-digger's toes," and "colder than a pawnbroker's smile" have also been heard.

Cowhands have described their personal discomforts due to cold weather by declaring that "I'm blue as a whetstone"; "I'm shiverin' like a dog in a briar patch"; "I'm shakin' like a dog in a blue norther"; "I'm shiverin' like a range-starved cow in a Panhandle norther"; "I'm shakin' like a Chihuahua pup with a chill"; and "I'm shiverin' like a lizard lookin' for a hot rock." A cold object might be spoken of as "cold as frog legs," or "cold as a dead snake."

Hot weather also comes in for its share of vivid descriptions. "Hot as election day in a hornet's nest"; "hot as the backlog of hell"; "hotter'n the hubs of hell"; and "hotter'n hell with the blower on" are examples. Ace Eaton used to say, "The weather's so hot it'd slip hair on a bear"; and once I heard another declare that the weather was "so hot and dry you had to prime yourself to spit."

I remember Jack Toliver once describing himself as being "as hot as the underside of a saddle blanket after a hard ride"; and on another occasion Hoot Perry said he was "hotter'n a burnt boot." Charlie Nelms described a tenderfoot dressed up in hairy chaps and other cowboy leather with, "From the hair he's wearin' you'd think it's cold 'nough to make a polar bear hunt cover, but it's hot as hell with the blower on." Another spoke of the heat that "sweated me down like a tallow candle."

Stormy Davis, speaking of the desert country, once expressed his opinion of that section with the comment that "there's just a thin sheet of sandpaper between that country and hell." Whitey Blythe expressed the same opinion in different words with, "That country was so hot that if a man died there and went to hell he'd wire back for blankets." Fuzzy Rogers' way of speaking of another section was, "It's so hot it'd make hell look like an icebox." I heard Shell Patterson tell of a section in Arizona where the natives, with civic pride, tried to convince him that the heat was in his imagination. "But," he ended, "when the prunes begin stewin' in their own juice, I'll say it's hot." Another puncher, telling of an experience in a hot country, declared that "if somebody'd a-stuck a fork in me they'd found me well done." Still another spoke of the weather being "so hot it'd take two hours to blow a cup of coffee cool."

Drouths came in for their share of vigorous expressions. Following a long drouth the condition of the country was spoken of as being "dry as a covered bridge"; "drier'n a cork leg"; "dry as a Methodist sermon"; and you would likely hear some complaints about the range not being "able to support a horned frog." One day during an unusually dry summer, while riding over the range inspecting the fast drying waterholes, Silk Kutner declared, "There ain't 'nough grass in the whole state to winter a prairie dog." On a similar occasion I heard Shanks Malloy state that "there ain't 'nough grass to chink the crack between the ribs of a sandfly." During a drouth one cowboy observed, "The cattle was so thin they looked like they had only one gut." Another said it was "so dry a grass widow wouldn't take root." On the old T Anchor one cowboy exaggerated the fact that it "hasn't rained since Noah," and he had "forgot what water looked like outside a pail or trough." To one cowhand the weather "was dry as popcorn."

The foreman of the Ox Bow, studying the cloudless sky for sign, predicted that "another month without rain and we'll have a herd of jerky on the hoof." Dunk Stevens made a ride through a country where there "wasn't 'nough grass to wad a smooth-bore gun," and dismounting at the home ranch, he thirstily declared he was "drier'n jerked buffalo with an empty water barrel." He had gone down in the lower country to inspect the river, but brought back the discouraging news that "the river bed's as dry as a tobacco box."

When the rains did come, the cowman, as with every other phase of his life, did not lack for salty expressions. In telling of a particularly hard rain, Dan Little ended by stating that "after that gully-washer it was wet 'nough to bog a snipe." John Banning expressed the same thought when he said that "the whole country was so swampy it'd bog a butterfly." On one rainy roundup when the boys were having trouble with slick, muddy boots trying to fork horses that spooked at the crackling yellow slickers, Rang Fifer stated disgustedly that "this weather'd drown a duck with an umbrella tail." "It rained so long ever'body wished they'd grown fins instead of feet," was Poverty Engle's way of describing a long rainy spell; and I once heard Luke Leeds picture a ride up a certain clay hill which was, as he said, "slick as calf slobbers."

When such weather, as one cowboy said, "gets plumb wholesale," it got "boggy 'nough to bog a buzzard's shadow"; or a rider would get "bogged to the saddle skirts." I heard one cowboy, after a long drouth, say he "hoped it rains hard 'nough so we have to dive down to grease the windmills."

The cowboy has many unique expressions for his descriptions of anyone or anything poor in flesh. In speaking of the range cattle after an extended drouth, Abe Combs observed that "they looked like the runnin' gear of a katydid"; and on another occasion one made a similar description when he said, "Some of those steers were so thin you could look right through 'em and read the Lord's Prayer." Another spoke of an orphan calf as being "just a ball of hair." And others have used such phrases as "poorer than a leppy calf at a dry waterhole"; "poor as a whip-o-will"; "gant as a gutted snowbird"; "lean as a desert grasshopper"; and "thin as a cow in April." Bob Terrell described a poor calf as "so poor he looked like a ball of hair with a butcher knife run through it."

A person who had noticeably lost weight might be described as "fallin' off like persimmons after a frost"; and I remember another cowhand, in speaking of a sick spell he had just experienced, saying, "When I shook loose from the piggin' string of that fever I'd shore lost a layer of fat off my ribs." Pat Young spoke of another as being "so poor his shadow was developin' holes in it"; while Silvertip Reed described another such person as being "so thin you couldn't hit him with a handful of loose corn." Jesse Spillers once said of a thin person that "he's built like a snake on stilts and has to stand twice to make a shadow"; while to Trav Lambert "he's about as fat as a stall-fed knittin' needle" better expressed his idea of a thin person. One spoke of a real thin person as "so narrow he could take a bath in a shotgun barrel"; and Cal Mason said of another that "if he'd close one eye he'd look like a needle." Another might be "so lank he could take the slack hide of his belly and use it for a hand-kerchief."

Ed Pearson said of one, "He's so thin he has to lean against a saplin' to cuss"; and I have heard others described as "so thin you couldn't notch him in the sights of a saddle gun"; "so thin his hide flaps on his bones like a bedquilt on a ridgepole"; and "so poor and pale he looked like he was just walkin' 'round to save funeral expenses." Another spoke of one being "so thin it looked like we'd have to tail him up."

A weak person was said to be "paper backed," and if he was soft it was "like he was built of butter." It was also said of a puny person that "he couldn't lick his upper lip"; and Pack Mears said of one, "He's so puny he couldn't pull my hat off." Jim Houston referred to a sickly man as being "weak as a dragged cat," and Breezy Flynn spoke of another as being "so weak a kitten's robust beside him." Bud Cowan once told me of a "lunger" visiting his ranch in search of health, and he ended his description of the invalid by saying, "His lungs wasn't stronger than a hummin' bird's, and he didn't have 'nough wind to blow out a candle," and he added that "his cough sounded like an overture to a funeral." In speaking of others who felt badly, the cowboy was apt to say that "he's off his feed."

I once heard a cowman describe a tall man as "so tall it'd take a steeplejack to look him in the eye." Frijole Holt said of another, "He's shore built high above his corns"; and Stud Mayfield described another as being "so long he has to shorten his stirrups to keep from wearin' out his boot soles." Speedy Ford spoke of another as being "so tall he couldn't tell when his feet were cold"; and another was said to "wear his pockets high off the ground."

To the cowboy a very short man "drags the ground when he walks," or he might "have to borrow a ladder to kick a gnat on the ankle." Of another is was said that "he had to have a box to mount his hoss." I once heard one describing a girl he had just met with, "She ain't ankle high to a June bug." Another cowhand was described as being "so short he couldn't see over a sway-backed hoss"; and still another as "so short he looks like he's sawed off at the pockets." One shorty was described as having "to take up his stirrups on a man-sized saddle," and of another it was said that "he wasn't the size to brag without a box to stand on." A short object was often expressed as being "as short as the tail hold on a bear."

To be "square" or "onto his business" had a very broad meaning on the range. A man entitled to such testimonials to his worth had to possess the qualities of unflinching courage, of daring, of self-reliance; and with these he had to be ready and willing to "stand by" a brother cowman and do his duty efficiently in everything that might happen to come up in the work of the day. Moreover, whatever he might have been elsewhere, he must be truthful, honest and honorable in all his relations to the outfit as a whole and to each of the men with whom he was associated in taking care of its property. Lying, crookedness and double-dealing were intolerable offenses in that close-bound life.

Such a man was said to be "as straight as a wagon tongue," or "he stands as up and down as a cow's tail." No higher compliment could be paid a man than to say of him that "he'll do to ride the river with." I once heard Pack Mears refer to a man with, "His word's as bindin' as a hangman's knot on a hossthief's neck"; and such expressions as "he's sixteen hands high," and "his heart's as straight as a rifle barrel" have been heard. An honest man was either "honest as a woman's lookin' glass," or "as open-faced as a Waterbury watch."

In looking over my notes I find a liberal collection of expressions used by the cowboy to signify his idea of meanness, or of someone being or looking mean. These various phrases may be heard around any campfire where booted riders gather.

To the cowman a downright mean person would "eat off the same plate with a snake," and was, in his opinion, "lowdown 'nough to pack a bucket of sheepdip." Noisy Leach once described such a person as "so tough he's growed horns and is haired over"; and Cleve Bender spoke of another being "so tough he had to sneak up on the dipper to get a drink of water." Jed Larson used to tell of a ranch down in New Mexico where the "whole crew was tougher'n a basket of snakes," and the old man himself

"looked so wicked he's shore of a reserved seat in hell."
John Banning of the Jigger Y used to tell of a character
who was "meaner'n a centipede with the chilblains, and
don't have no more conscience than a cow in a stampede."
Pima Norton described another as being "tougher'n the
callouses on a barfly's elbow." At another time he spoke
of a man having "snake blood and bein' about as sociable
as an ulcerated tooth."

Latigo Tate told a story of a man who "claims he's
the toughest longhorn that ever shakes his antlers in Arizona," and he further stated that he really turned out to be
"as full of venom as a rattlesnake in August." Rawhide
Gilson used a similar description in referring to a man who
"was poisonous as any reptile as ever made a track in the
sand." "He looked meaner'n a new-sheared sheep," said
Curt Meyers on one occasion in describing a man; and
Tucson Williams spoke of another as being "mean tem-
pered as a cow camp cook before breakfast"; while Tom
Kirk spoke of another by saying, "He's a wolf and he ain't
togged out in no sheep wool either."

Lippy Yeagen described a quarrelsome person as "so
disagreeable a shepherd dog couldn't get 'long with him."
In one of his tales about the Dry Cimarron country Cal
Griffin referred to a certain killer as being "cold-blooded
as a rattler with a chill." One old gunman used to brag
that his "family tree was a scrub and he was Old Man
Trouble's only son." In speaking of a section of Oklahoma, Pete Dunbar said, "That country's so tough the
hoot owls all sing bass"; and another spoke of a certain
gunman as being "tough as a sow's snout." Puddin' Spof-
ford, in speaking of some horses in his string, claimed,
"Them broncs are as mean as gar soup thickened with
tadpoles."

The cowboy is not lacking in phrases to express his
opinion of crookedness either. I have heard many such

assertions as "he's as crooked as a snake in a cactus patch"; "he's so crooked his hair is kinky"; and "he's so crooked a rattler'd break his back trailin' him." Snuffles Hill once described a man "so crooked he could swaller nails and spit out corkscrews."

In speaking of a bad horse, one cowhand remarked, "I never saw so much hell wrapped up in one hoss hide." Another, telling of a mean, wild bull they had been having trouble with, said, "You never know the meanness that's planned below the horn wrinkles of that old moss-back." Crookedness has also been described with such terms as "he's crooked 'nough to sleep on a corkscrew"; "he's so crooked he could sleep in the shade of a posthole auger"; or "he's so crooked he has to screw on his socks." A mean person might be "meaner'n a rattlesnake in a hot skillet"; "tougher'n a basket of snakes"; or "just plumb cultus."

In describing a man he did not like, one cowhand said, "He's just as long as a snake and drags the ground when he walks"; and another said of such a man that "his biography would have to be written on asbestos paper." Describing an old maid, Hank Travers observed, "She was soured on life and couldn't get the acid from her system."

There is no prouder soul on earth than the cowman. A horseman has always felt himself to be better than the man on foot, and has contempt for the man who walks. To the cowboy it is a disgrace to follow a plow, which he calls "lookin' at a mule's tail"; and in his own words, he is "too proud to cut hay and not wild 'nough to eat it."

Much of his pride is in the ranch, not its owner. If asked where he works, he will not say he works for a certain man or firm, but will say he is "ridin' for the Lazy Y brand," or is "punchin' for the Wagonwheel outfit." Of course, if he is riding for some "little three-up outfit that don't own 'nough beef to hold a barbeque" he is not "any prouder'n a lost sheepherder."

The cowboy is proud of his gear and rigging if he has a good outfit, so perhaps he has a right to be "swelled up like a carbuncle." On one occasion I heard Swing Harper speak of a man as being "prouder than a road runner," or "struttin' like a turkey gobbler in a hen pen"; and at a later time another puncher made the statement that a certain man was "swelled up like a frog in a churn." One cowboy said of a man that "he's swelled up till he busted his surcingle"; while another described a proud individual as being "as full of pride as a bull is of wind in corn time"; and another haughty man was said to be "walkin' like a dog had pissed on his leg"; or, as one said, "He's walkin' like a cat on mud."

The average cowhand "has a heart in his brisket as big as a saddle blanket," and is generous to a fault. Nothing he owns is too good to share with a fellow puncher if this puncher needs it. Let him hear of some rider being sick and broke and needing medicine and the whole range would empty its pockets.

But a stingy person was scornfully said to be "stingy 'nough to skin a flea for its hide and tallow." Dunk Lanton once told of a fellow who "was so stingy that if he owned a lake he wouldn't give a duck a drink"; and on another occasion Grady Dennis told of one who "wouldn't give a dollar to see an earthquake." On another range it was said of the owner of a one-horse outfit that "he'd squeeze a dollar till the eagle started losin' flesh"; and Sandy Vance further enlightened me that "he wouldn't give a nickel for a front seat at the Battle of Waterloo." Cleve Mulhall described a rider with whom he had worked as being "one of those fellers that after you'd shared a bedroll with him for a couple of months, you felt like you knew him well 'nough to borrow a match."

Other expressions I have heard concerning parsimony are: "He wouldn't give a meat-rind to grease a griddle"; "he's so stingy he wouldn't chew tobacco because he'd have to spit"; and "he'd chase a tomtit to hell for a pumpkin seed and spoil a good knife cuttin' him open." In describing an old sheepherder, Ted Foster said, "He comes to town with a dirty shirt and a dollar bill and he don't change neither while he's there"; and another told of a tightwad wagon boss "so stingy Injuns wouldn't go near his wagon." Still another said of a stingy person that "he's tight as a bull's ass in fly time."

The cowman encouraged fruitfulness in his cattle, but when it came to the human family he did not look upon it with much favor. He left that to the nester. Tom Garver told of a nester that "shore kept the stork flyin' till the sawbones made a plain trail goin' to his shack." At a later time I heard another puncher say of a man that "by the number of descendants he's got he musta been a Bishop in Utah." Henry King told of one who "had so many offspring he had to buy a wagon"; and another spoke of the growing family of a certain nester with, "He's got four kids and another in the shops." Some plentiful object was sometimes spoken of as being "plentiful as ticks in a wet spring."

The cowboy was apt to describe something scarce as being "scarce as hiccups at a prayer meetin'"; "scarce as upper teeth in a cow"; "scarce as hen's teeth"; or "scarce as grass around a windmill."

An unpopular person was spoken of as being as "popular as a tax collector"; "as popular as a wet dog at a parlor social"; while his company was "as welcome as a rattler in a dog town"; or was "as welcome as a polecat at a picnic"; "as popular as one strange bulldog to another"; "as popular as a bastard calf in a bull herd"; or "as polite as a hound to a stray dog after his bone." "He's an unpopular as a bear in a pigpen," was another such phrase; or if he had worn out his welcome it was said "his cinch was gettin' frayed."

A popular man was said to "have more friends than there's fiddlers in hell"; and a person or thing might be "as popular as a snake in a prohibition town," or "popular as a pat straight flush." The cowboy also had ways of expressing his idea of being welcome as in the phrase, "He was as welcome as Santa Claus in an orphan asylum."

Though profane, and capable of language "that would peel the hide off a Gila monster," the old-time cowman was not without his religion. He had small opportunity to attend church, but through his knowledge of nature and the great outdoors, he knew there was a Higher Being. During the nights on roundup when he lay out in the open he studied the heavenly bodies and perhaps felt more closely kin to God than the city man with all his churches. Even when he did have the opportunity to go to town, he did not want to spend this rare freedom "listenin' to psalm singin' and exhortations on sin." He had no use for some "double-dyed hypocrite," as one said, "who tried to pull himself out of a hole by gettin' down on his prayer-bones and taffyn' the Lord up." It might be said of him that "most of his religion was in his wife's name"; and as one said of a religious man, "He was raised on prunes and proverbs."

I heard one old-timer speak of a certain sinner with, "He's been flounderin' in the mire of sin so long old St. Peter wouldn't recognize him as a candidate for wings." Another admitted that he "wasn't pickin' any grapes in the Lord's Vineyard." One old-timer admitted that "at the final showdown I don't want to be left out to starve on a bare range"; and another said he "wanted to be up yonder where there was no end of harps and free music."

The cowboy was an inveterate cigarette smoker. If there ever was a badge of a calling it should be the little Bull Durham tag hanging by its yellow string from the vest or shirt pocket. I have heard several descriptions of a cowboy preparing to roll a smoke such as "he strolled outside with a bag of Bull Durham in one hand while he gophers through his vest for papers with the other"; and "he jerked a leaf out of his prayer book [what he calls his book of cigarette papers] and commenced building a new life of Bull Durham."

He did not have much taste for a pipe, but left that tobacco furnace to the sheepherder, the nester and the prospector. Dick Blocker described a pipe-smoking individual as "makin' more smoke than a wet wood fire"; and Duke Noel spoke of another "puffin' a pipe so strong it'd derail a freight train."

The cowboy had many ways of describing something slick. I have heard such apt figures as: "slick as calf slobbers"; "slick as an eel in olive oil"; "slick as a gun barrel"; "slicker than a blue clay hill after a rainstorm"; "slick as spit on a doorknob"; "slick as a saddle rope"; and "slick as a schoolmarm's knee."

# Roundin' Up the Strays

THE COWBOY of the brush country was different from the Plains cowboy. He dressed and worked differently, used a shorter rope, and used tapaderos on his stirrups, but he spoke the same lingo and used the same salty idioms.

Skeeter Mays seemed to be proud of the fact that he "came from down in that country where the brush was so thick the birds couldn't fly through it and the snakes had to climb to see out," and he told it at every opportunity. Another "limbskinner" also used to brag that he was from a section where "the brush was so thick the birds couldn't build nests in it." I once heard Nub Elkins tell of a brush rider who "came out of that brush with 'nough wood hangin' to the horn of his saddle to cook a side of yearlin' ribs." One Plains cowboy who did not like the brush country commented, "To ride through that brush a man needed one of them suits built by a blacksmith."

When speaking of a large brand, the cowhand is likely to use such expressions at Totem Byers did when he said, "That steer's wearin' a brand so big you could read it in the moonlight"; or, as Bill Dugan once remarked, "You could've spotted that brand through a hoss-blanket." I once heard another speak of a brand "as big as a patent medicine sign."

I think it was Skinner West who, upon seeing a horse covered with brands, said, "That hoss is burnt till he looks like a brand book." An animal so branded tells a story of many owners with no friends among any of them. It is a pretty good sign he is a bad and worthless horse. Most all cowmen know the brands of their section, and at a dance, for instance, one might be out looking the horses over "to check on the brands to see who's arrived." One cowhand, referring to the branding crew at work, said that "they're busy burnin' and trimmin' up calves."

Most cowboys are crazy about dances and will ride many miles to attend one. They called these dances "hoe-digs," "hoe-downs," "shindigs," or "stomps." Dancing was said to be "stormin' the puncheons," "shakin' a fetlock," or "shakin' a hoof." When one said he was "makin' the calico crack," he meant that he was swinging his partner off the floor until her long dress popped like "crackin' the whip."

An apt description of the caller at a dance was that "he was a man with leather lungs and a loud mouth," and another described him as having "his head reared back like a coffee-pot lid" when he called. It was said of the fiddler that "he's shore makin' that fiddle talk a language that puts ginger in your feet." One old-timer said, "Dancin' in them days wasn't just wigglin' 'round and shakin' your rump. It was a rompin', stompin' affair."

Some churchgoing older man, after hearing this blood-stirring fiddle music, couldn't stand such temptations and, as one said, "He don't need no invite to dance himself right out of the church." Many cowhands, after a few dances, "were cussin' the blisters on their heels and the new boots that caused them, but they're not missin' a dance, even if their feet are on fire." After the dance was over, the men were apt "to throw a stag dance that's likely to be kinda rough and end up in a wrestlin' match," and, as another said, "with their feet feelin' like they'd wintered on a hard pasture."

The average cowhand has little use for a braggart and of such a character it might be said that "he got callouses from pattin' his own back"; "he's all gurgle and no guts"; or "he bragged himself out of a place to lean against a bar."

The cowboy's idea of being lonely might be expressed with such a phrase as "lonely as a teetotaler in a saloon." To describe someone who had no chance of winning, a cowhand might say, "He stood about as much show as a hen at a mass meetin' of coyotes." To take to something might be expressed with such phrases as: "He takes to it as mild as milk"; "he takes to it like a bear to bee tree"; or "he takes to it like honeysuckle to a front porch."

When Jud Cramer spoke of taking a chance with a situation, he said, "I had to play that hand with my eyes shut"; and another cowhand described a similar situation with, "He was grabbin' the brandin' iron by the hot end." Speaking of recognizing someone or remembering him, I once heard a cowhand declare, "I'd know him in hell with his hide burnt off"; and another stated, "I'd know his ashes in a whirlwind."

It was said of a meddler who "horned in" on something which did not concern him that he was one of those "eye-ballers that's always feedin' off his own range." When a cowman only touched a subject on the edges, he was said to be "coyotin' 'round the rim." Something fragile "wouldn't hold no more'n a cobweb would a cow." "Buffaloed" meant mentally confused, as well as meaning to strike one in the head with a six-gun. "Coyotin' 'round" was sneaking; "campin' on his trail" meant following someone; "lookin' for a dog to kick" was to be disgusted; "airin' his lungs" was cursing; "airin' the paunch" was vomiting; and "washin' out the canyon" was taking a bath. "Staked to a fill" was to be given a good meal; "blow in with the tumbleweeds" was to come unexpectedly; a determined man had "hell in his neck"; to "rib up" was to persuade; "stood up" meant robbed; and "calf around" or "soak" was the cowboy's expression for loafing, while "sweat" was to work for board without other pay.

A cowboy never spoke of carrying anything, but always "packed" it, as "packed a gun," or "packed his saddle." To him late afternoon meant in the "shank of the afternoon." "Light" meant to dismount from a horse; a "jamboree" might be anything from a dance or a drinking party to a gunfight or a stampede. "Mix the medicine" was a phrase of Indian origin. To some Indians, "medicine" was any procedure that procured the results he desired, whether in disease, war, love, hunting, fishing or farming. "No medicine" meant that he had no information. One cowboy, describing a group who had squatted down for a confab, said, "They hunkered down on their ⎷ boot heels to take comfort in a frog squat." It would have been much simpler to just say they "squatted down to talk."

A tactless person was said to have "no more tact than a bull goin' through a fence." Jud Mason told of a rider who had been thrown from his horse quite a distance from the ranch and was forced to walk back when his horse ran away. "He terrapined his way back to camp," said Jud, "and by the time he'd got there he'd lost considerable steam and was whistlin' like a wind-broke hoss." In a similar situation, another spoke of one out of breath as "blowin' like a bull snake at a barkin' dog." Of such another runaway horse a cowboy said, "He gets homesick for his own feed trough and high-tails it for home."

To the cowboy, comfort was "cozy as a toad under a cabbage leaf"; while something unpleasant was "about as refreshin' as bein' burned at stake." His idea of sourness was "so sour it'd pucker a pig's mouth"; and a careless person was described as being "careless as a cow walkin' through standin' grass." Something unnoticeable or of small consequence "didn't attract as much attention as an empty bottle." When a man was killed out on the range and left unburied he was said to make "a free lunch counter for the coyotes"; a cautious person was said to be "as aloof as a mountain sheep"; and when one cowboy heard another snoring in his sleep, he described him as "snorin' like a choked bull" — just a few more examples of the cowman's unique yet apt descriptions. The cowboy was apt to describe an awkward person as being "clumsy as a foundered mare"; an unlucky person as being as "out of luck as a woodpecker in a petrified forest"; it might be said of a peevish or ill-tempered person that "he's got more crust than an armadillo"; a serious person was "serious as a kid pullin' out a splinter." An apprehensive person might be said to be "nervous as a prostitute in church," or "nervous as a dog dreamin' of rats."

A contented person might be "purrin' like a tomcat in a creamery"; while an inquisitive person might be "nosey as a ring-tail coon." One cowboy described a bucking horse as "pitchin' stiff-legged as a mad ostrich"; or it might be said of someone who had failed in an accomplishment that "he couldn't flag down a gut wagon," "he couldn't head a hobbled goose in a lane," or "he couldn't hide no more than a hill."

Jim Brady, describing a bunch of cowboys attending a ranch dance, said, "They'd run in a straight steer herd so long they're shy as a green bronc to a new water trough when 'round women." Another told of the cook's ability to dig out the lead from a cowhand who had received a bullet in his leg with the comment, "He's right there with a parin' knife when it comes to minin' for lead." In speaking of tall grass, the cowboy might say that "the grass was belly deep to a camel," or "that grass was belly deep to a tall coon on a mule." He might describe his idea of one smiling by saying that "he's smilin' like a nigger eatin' watermelon," or "he had a smile on his face that'd water a hoss." Something messed up would be as "messed up as a grass rope on a wet mornin'," or "he messed up things worse'n a red hen in a pile of cow manure."

When a cowhand told of a friend who ran a little ranch in Oklahoma, he said, "He runs a little cockle-bur outfit down on the Cimarron." Another told of a cowhand who was "workin' for a little three-up spread that don't own much more'n a cowpen herd"; and another cowboy said of a small rancher that "he don't own 'nough cattle to hold a barbecue." Tom Thacher described a nester boy as "one of them two-buckle boys that looks at a mule's tail all day." One cowboy spoke of a friend who had gone into a city barbershop to experience his first manicure with, "He's havin' his forehoofs roached and rasped by a pink and white filly."

Most of the early cowmen had a poor opinion of bankers, and one, describing such a man, commented that "a banker is a feller who loans you an umbrella when the sun's shinin' and wants it back pronto when it starts to sprinkle." It was said of a boy who had grown up on a ranch that "he just growed up with the rest of the yearlin's." Ted McGaw had a unique way of telling of another cowhand who had just fallen into the river, and when he got out he lay on the bank and "pointed his feet toward Jesus to let the water run out of his boots."

A cowhand once described another's saddle as "one of them round-skirted saddles that looked like an old hen with her tail feathers pulled out." Another told of a companion being so thirsty that "he walked right into the river so he could drink standin' up." I once heard another describe a whirlpool in a stream by saying, "It's spinnin' 'round like the button on a privy door." An enthusiastic person might be described as being "as enthusiastic as an Apache squaw with a hundred feet of beef guts." A bunch of cowhands mounted on the top rail of a corral fence to watch the riding of a bad horse was described as being "lined up on the top rail like a bunch of fool hens on a spruce limb."

Something handy was "handier'n a vest pocket." Tom Booth, telling of a fellow puncher who quit punching cows, added, "After he quit the range he got a job down on the Rio Grande as a chili chaser." He meant that the one spoken of had taken a job as border patrolman to keep Mexicans from crossing into the United States unlawfully. Another old-timer told of the days of his youth and referred to it as "away back when hell was frosty and the jackrabbits still wore horns." Someone jumping up and down was described as "jumpin' like a speckled-legged frog from a dry hole." When a crowd of cowboys came riding into town in a hurry, it was said that "they flocked in like cattle to a water-hole durin' a drouth."

A trustful person might be described as "unsuspectin' as a deacon at a camp meetin'"; of a person in need of something it might be said that "he needs it worse than a scalded pup needs a snowbank." When a man came West "just two steps ahead of the sheriff" he was apt to change his name and it was said that "he drew a new name from the pack"; anything fertile was said to be "fertile as a gambler's brain"; and something simple was "simple as the sight on a gun."

The cowboy's idea of something being impregnable was "as invincible as four aces and a king"; one described a mountain trail as being "so steep it looked like a beaver-slide."

In telling of a ranch woman petting and making over a small boy, Joe Harper said, "She's fussin' over him like a sagehen over a wild goslin'." Something monotonous might be "as monotonous as a naggin' woman." In telling of a fat man who fell into the river, Doak Turner said that "he dried up the river for fifty feet when he landed." Another, speaking of a fellow puncher being killed in a stampede, remarked, "Those sharp hoofs chopped him up real fine to save on funeral expenses"; and someone unwilling was said to be "as unwillin' as a bridegroom at a shotgun weddin'." To Joe Dawson something noisy was "noisy as a blue jay camp meetin'."

When nesters began moving in around his ranch, an old-timer declared, "The country's gettin' plumb full of pumpkin pilers." Another spoke of the town loafers he always saw when he went to town with, "It always did rile a workin' cowhand when he saw them town porch perchers." In speaking of the lack of sleep one got while on the trail, one cowhand said: "If you reach down and find your clothes cold, you've overslept." During a thunderstorm with lightning flashing every few seconds, an old-timer commented, "The Ole Man up there's stompin' out his campfire and the sparks are flyin'." After drinking some gyp water, one cowhand observed, "That gyp water's so mean it'd run uphill and wouldn't stay in a jug." Something long might be expressed as "long as a rustler's dream." "He tries to Injun up on that maniac den," was the way one cowboy described another trying to sneak up on a sheep wagon. When a cowboy was arrested because he was trying to shoot up the town, and was asked his purpose in creating this disturbance, he answered, "I just wanted to have my fun before that old feller with the hay-hook comes 'long."

Something that gave little shade was said to "give 'bout as much shade as a bob-wire fence." When a cowhand said of another that "they shook a rope at him," he meant that the one spoken of had been warned of the error of his ways. It was said of a man doing any chore to make an honest living that he was trying "to keep the wolf from havin' pups on his doorstep." Something that filled quickly "filled up like a water-hole in April." How unique, yet fitting, to describe a man who had just slipped out of sight by saying, "He leaked out of the landscape"; and when there was some doubt in a person's mind as to whether he could win in an endeavor it was said that "it made him look at his hole card."

When one cowboy was thrown from his horse and left afoot a long way from home, he said: "There's more of hell above the ground than I thought." Another, telling of a crooked trail he had just traveled, stated, "That trail was crookeder than a privy door latch." Still another described a section of country noted for its crime and killings as "a section where the sheriff and doctors were kept busy." A man using an old worn-out and ragged saddle was described by one cowboy as "using one of them saddles that eats both ways." Something of no consequence to one might be described with, "It means no more to him than fallen arches to an angleworm." Of one playing while in a relaxed and playful mood it might be said that "he's playin' like a kid in rompers"; or of one grinning that "he's grinnin' like a possum eatin' yellow jackets."

Something which spread quickly was apt to be described as "spreadin' like a grass fire"; when a group of men jumped through a saloon door in a hurry to avoid being in the line of fire of a shooting match inside, a witness said that "they dived out of that saloon like tree frogs"; and when one was riled up to a fighting mood, he was said to have "humped his back like a hog goin' to war." One cowhand described a city restaurant as "one of them places with thick tableware and thin soup." Another who had been employed by the same ranch for many years stated, "I figger I've been with this spread long 'nough to be entitled to a warm corner."

It might be said of anyone who seemed able to accomplish anything he attempted that "he could raise hair on a currycomb"; and one who seemed to have a talent for stirring up trouble might be described with, "He churns up a lot of dust." When a cowboy yells, he is said to "let out a yell that'd drive a wolf to suicide"; when one attacks another quickly it might be said that "he swoops down on him like forty hen hawks on a settin' quail"; and something which gave one away "gave him away like a shirtful of fleas."

The cowboy's intimate conversation is itself distinctive. Pithy, terse sentences are expected of him; in a lively group the conversation sometimes sparkles with a quick, slangy wit. Such original combinations as I have cited have won for some Westerners a pleasing notoriety.

Writers have for many years been telling us about the "passing of the cowboy." True, his field of activity has been more and more cramped, but we still have him with us. The wire fence has changed many of his methods of working; the advance of civilization has changed much of his picturesque style in dress and accouterments, but his language has been bred in him. The present-day cowboy speaks the same language as his earlier brother and he will cling to this lingo as long as men handle cattle. It fits his calling and is his "mother tongue." It is a part of him, a part which modern civilization has been unable to despoil.

Picturesque as are the many languages of the world, there is none more distinctive, more individual, than the lingo of the American cowboy. His phraseology is original with him alone, the outcome of his own experience. While Webster slights many words used on the frontier, to the frontiersman they are highly useful and exact in description. If one attempts to put his speech into correct English he would only succeed in destroying its strength and flavor.

From the time of our early settlement upon the edge of civilization the frontiersman has felt free from convention and social restrictions, and he carried this into his speech. Living in a world of reality and practicality, his speech has utilized simple terms of comparison and figure, and these qualities have added a delightful saltiness. Taking the salt from the cowboy's speech would be like failing to put it in the steaks he raises — leaving it tasteless and unpalatable. To me there is nothing more appealing than the jargon of this individual when he is among his own kind, and I hope I never become stupid enough to resist it.

Cowhands are neither so plentiful nor so picturesque as they were in the days of the open range, and with the passing of its customs, many of their terms are becoming obsolete. This volume is an attempt to preserve this lingo for posterity. As long as we are a nation of meat-eaters I am not afraid that the cowboy himself will become extinct, but some of his older language may die with the passing years. However, he will create new idioms typical of the range as long as he forks a horse. Furthermore, living in the tradition of men who ride semi-wild horses to work obstinate, unruly cattle, he will never become so soft that he will pack a lunch, wear his sleeves rolled up, and say *my gracious* instead of *goddam* when he is mad.